This is a story about an ordinary man who has had an extraordinary life. It is hard to believe the hand that life has dealt me, but I am still here doing my bit.

*Jacqui,
Thanks for your support*

B...

My Life Story
The Real Life of Brian

BRIAN WINSTANLEY

My Life Story
The Real Life of Brian

Vanguard Press

VANGUARD PAPERBACK

© Copyright 2016
Brian Winstanley

The right of Brian Winstanley to be identified as author of
this work has been asserted by him in accordance with the
Copyright, Designs and Patents Act 1988.

All Rights Reserved

No reproduction, copy or transmission of this publication
may be made without written permission.
No paragraph of this publication may be reproduced,
copied or transmitted save with the written permission of the publisher,
or in accordance with the provisions
of the Copyright Act 1956 (as amended).

Any person who commits any unauthorised act in relation to
this publication may be liable to criminal
prosecution and civil claims for damages.
A CIP catalogue record for this title is
available from the British Library.

Although the author and publisher have made every effort to ensure that the
information in this book was correct at press time, the author and publisher do not
assume and hereby disclaim any liability to any party for any loss, damage, or
disruption caused by errors or omissions, whether such errors or omissions result
from negligence, accident, or any other cause.

ISBN 9781784650858

Vanguard Press is an imprint of
Pegasus Elliot MacKenzie Publishers Ltd.

www.pegasuspublishers.com

First Published in 2016

Vanguard Press
Sheraton House Castle Park
Cambridge England

Printed & Bound in Great Britain

Acknowledgements

I would like to thank my many friends and relations for all the help and support they have given me, especially in my darkest hours.

I would also like to thank the doctors and nurses at; Brighton Royal Sussex County Hospital, Worthing Hospital, Chichester Hospital, Brighton General Hospital, Haywards Health Hospital, Southlands Hospital, and not forgetting the amazing Stoke Mandeville Hospital and Glebelands Day Centre.

Lastly and most importantly, I would like to thank my wonderful wife, Jackie, who has been on this journey with me and put up with me along the way.

I would also like to give a special thanks to my daughter, Karan, for sitting for hours translating my scribbling and making it legible. Without her help, this book would still be in my head.

"What a book! About an amazing brave gentleman, who has had so much pain throughout his life. He has given so much back to others and still does. Feel blessed to know you Brian."

Independent – Catherine Lister

Who is Brian Winstanley? Where do I start?

Born in Godstone, Surrey on the 12th August 1941, the young Brian was oblivious to which direction his incredible life would take him.

Well, this amazing man was like a cat… yes, really; he was fearless, athletic, took risks, and had a knack of dodging death by a whisker.

I met Brian through his wonderful, supportive and adoring wife, Jackie, who is a very dear friend of mine. When I was introduced to him, I was immediately aware of his amazing sense of humour, compassion and integrity. Now two years on, I realise that this is not all that makes Brian the man he is today.

He has experienced many challenges in his life and his determination and positivity have helped him succeed no matter what the situation. He is without doubt, as my husband calls him, "our super hero".

Despite everything, he is always there to lend a helping hand when needed. He works voluntarily with people with disabilities, and when my husband was seriously ill with a brian tumour, he did not hesitate in driving me regulary to the hospital to visit him.

Brian is a true friend and an extraordinary man. Life for him has not always been straightforward to say the least, and as you will read in his remarkable story; it has been challenging, funny, touching and always surprising.

So who is Brian Winstanley? He is like my bra – supportive, comfortable, lifts us up, and is always close to the heart.

Love you, "Super Hero".

Marian Hopwood

CHAPTER ONE

Well, after being pestered by my children for years, I am finally writing my story. I think you may find it interesting. I was born before the end of the war, 1941, despite Mr Hitler's efforts! My mother was evacuated to Godstone and I was born there but then she came back to Portslade where I grew up and spent most of my life. I don't remember my mother and I am afraid I don't even know her proper name. I know they used to call her Dolly and her maiden name was Young. Sadly she died when I was about three. My father did his best (bless him), not much fun raising four boys on your own. Two of my brothers were older than me, Frank and Colin, and one younger, Michael.

My school days were not the happiest days of my life, probably because I had a mop of curly ginger hair and I used to be picked on – at least I could threaten them with my two big brothers! I went to St Peter's Infants, Benfield, and finally Portslade Secondary Modern. There were very few buses or cars so we all walked to school rain or shine; you could say we were poor but then most people were! It was very different in those days, most people knew each other.

It was a caring community, they didn't have much but they would give you their last shilling.

We lived in a very small house in North Street, the front room had been converted into a jeweller's shop. I loved watching Bazil, the jeweller mending clocks, watches and jewellery. The street in which we lived was really the main High Street and was full of hustle and bustle. It wasn't very long; you could walk from one end to the other in ten minutes. There were dozens of shops, pubs, two churches and a cinema. The hustle and bustle was amazing, horse and carts, hand carts, in the summer the old ladies got a chair out on the pavement and chatted to passers-by. People used to leave their front doors open with no fear of being robbed. The noises and the smells will stay with me forever. There was a man that sold winkles and sprats, all kinds of fish. There was another who sharpened knives, choppers and scissors and of course the rag bone man. Every shop had a chair for the elderly or disabled customers. To go shopping was quite a social affair. There was one shop, it was very dark inside, the old lady sold second-hand clothes and shoes. She had a stoop and a big wart on her nose. We all thought that she was a witch. She used to suddenly appear from behind a pile of clothes as if by magic. I remember there was a bell under the mat that rang if you stepped on it. She also sold second-hand comics which were on the table. We had no money so we jumped over the mat, grabbed a couple and ran.

The whole street was very 'Open All Hours'. I recall one shop interested me greatly was the ironmonger's. You could buy nails, screws, candles, firewood, paraffin, pots, pans and virtually anything, even bars of carbolic soap. There was a bicycle shop on one corner, the floor was a kind of lino but was covered over the years with oil which softened it and thousands of ball bearings had been trodden into it. They were shiny and they sparkled like stars in the night sky. You could hire a bike for three pence or get yours repaired.

On Sundays we all got dressed up in our Sunday best. If you got dirty you were for the high jump! I remember after Church one Sunday (which was compulsory) my mates and I went for a walk down by the canal. I trod in some tar which stuck to the sole of my new shoe. I then thought I would scrape it off on one of the railings. As I rubbed it, of course the shoe came off and 'splash!' it promptly sank. I had to go home with one shoe; my dad went ape. Later in the day we went back down and retrieved the shoe. When we got home dad tried to dry it in the oven. Of course it curled up like a crisp, nothing to do but buy a new pair. I was sent to bed with no tea and a clip around the ear.

The canal was a big part of my childhood. In summer holidays we would go out at eight in the morning and get home at five p.m. If we were lucky we would cadge a lift on the ferry. There were three, the main one being for the gasworks' workers. It was about ten feet long and carried about fifteen to sixteen men to and from work. There were two private ferries, one owned by Mr Lamkin who also did boat repairs and the other by a Fred Harlot who did anything to make a living. I used to sit and talk to him for hours about the really old days, when they worked a day for a penny shovelling coal off the barges and his exploits as a fisherman. In his sheds he cut timber then chopped it and bundled it for kindling and sold it. He had a dozen or more rowing boats which he used to hire out by the hour (they used to leak like sieves and you were constantly bailing). If we could not get on the ferry we walked around the canal which took all day. We behaved like kids and caught crabs, tiddlers and lizards, climbed in and out of boats getting into trouble.

Over the other side of the harbour there were many remains of the old concrete war defences. All these slabs of concrete piled on top of each other formed all these tunnels. I cringe now to think about it but we used to crawl on our stomachs through these gaps – anything could have happened, we had no fear! Throwing stones at cans and bottles and generally having fun. Come lunchtime we would find a big ship and call up to them and they would beckon us up, and make us a bacon or sausage doorstep sandwich with a mug of tea. Today it would be unthinkable!

The canal was filthy in those days with oil and tar. Dead cats and dogs were often seen covered in crabs, bottles and lumps of wood. We would often prod and poke with sticks. How anything lived in that was amazing; there were prawns, eels, mullet and crabs. To catch any of these we got an old biscuit tin, put loads of small holes in the bottom and three holes around the side. These holes had a piece of string about a foot long which were then attached to a line. We would tie an old fish head (which we would get from the fisherman) in the middle and lower it in the water. The crabs and prawns would feed on the fish. We would pull it up and then they were in the tin!

There used to be some larger water tanks down by the steps which led to the ferry. These tanks had covers on the tops which were very rusty and we used to climb on the top, lay down and play boats with the bits of wood pushing them from one end to the other. This particular day we were doing this and the top gave way. I went straight through and luckily for me this feller was off to work and he dragged me out. No doubt I would definitely have drowned at this point in my life as I could not swim! I thanked him and went home soaking wet to a good talking to.

Hove Lagoon was also one of our haunts in the winter. They would drain it out and it would leave a little bit of water. We would get a sharp stick, wade in and try to spear a flat fish. There was the odd dab or sole in there but I don't think we caught many!

Even when it rained hard we still went out and played boat races with lollysticks and matchsticks in the gutter. We had holes in our shoes and spuds in our socks (holes). Wellies rubbed your legs sore, we had patches and darns in our clothes, we were right little street urchins!

Down at the docks they imported many different types of goods, one of these being raw chocolate. This was solid but in sacks, which they used to stack on trailers ready to be picked up by the lorries. Well, we used to sneak behind the back of these, get out our penknives and hack a lump of this just big enough to carry then we would leg it up to the beach. We would then scramble under an upturned boat and eat chocolate until we were nearly sick!

When we were kids we were always hungry. This is an extraordinary story but Portslade was quite run down and fairly dingy. Well one day this movie film crew turned up. They wanted to film in a little square, they wanted eight of us kids to play in the street. A couple had to play football but three of us had to sit in the gutter and eat jam sandwiches. I thought this was great and I was going to be a film star – the star of the movie was Zsa Zsa Gabor! But of course she was not there. The filming started at about four thirty and they were still filming us at six p.m. Well my dad was getting concerned because it was getting dark by then so he sent my older brother, Colin, to look for me. He must have heard about the filming but when he got there, there was a big crowd on the south side of the main road. There was a wall about four feet high. My brother climbed up on this to see over the crowd. The problem being on the other side of the wall there was sixty foot drop! Sod's law – it happened that someone nudged him and over he went. The ambulance was called but we found out later they had stopped and asked this young feller if he had seen anything; this feller turned out to be my brother! Apparently about fifteen feet from the bottom there was an asbestos roof. He fell through this and it broke his fall; he never had a scratch on him. Anyway the ambulance men took him home and the next day we had a visit from Zsa Zsa with a model aeroplane. After he fell the filming stopped and I believe the scene was cut from the film. I don't even remember the name of the film.

At the bottom of North Street there were two scrapyards. We used to climb through a hole in the fence and it was a wonderful adventure. We used to climb into a scrap motor and be Stirling Moss for an hour or get chased off by the owner. Anyway one day we climbed into this big tank and when we moved some stuff underneath we found some live bullets, which we stuffed in our pockets. We then went home pleased as punch. We went around my mate's house and into his shed. Well, being kids we didn't know any better. We got one of the bullets and put it in a vice, we then got a nail and a hammer – well I think you know the rest… We hit the centre of the bullet, there was an almighty flash and an even louder bang! We could not hear anything. His dad came running out of the house like a mad man shouting and screaming. Within minutes the police and my dad had turned up and we had to hand over all of our treasures and tell them where we found them. We also got the biggest telling off ever! Mind you it did not stop us going into the other scrapyard.

One day we found this old nissen hut covered with brambles and old scrap iron. Well we got the door open and inside it was like it was when the Home Guard had left. There were old tin helmets, army belts, coats and bags, my prize possession being a candle telephone. There was one bayonet but no guns or ammo, thank heaven else god knows what would have happened. We used to pick wild rhubarb and eat it and poo for a week!

My father (who I haven't mentioned much) was a lovely hard working man. He was a builder by trade, he liked a pint and had a fag. He was one of the old school and thought children should be seen and not heard. He was very strict and would not suffer fools and bullshitters. He was very good at his job which was a Tacker (fixing plasterboard ceilings). He could also turn his hand to about anything. Well he decided to go upmarket and do away with the tin bath in front of the fire and so he acquired this white bath. The only place he could fit it was in the scullery, which was just inside the front door to the left. He had to knock out the old copper, which meant we had to take the washing down to the bag wash. Anyway the bath had the waste pipe connected but we had this huge big geyser; a huge water heater. When lit it would erupt with a huge woomah and dust and bits of plaster would fall off the ceiling. The only thing that separated the bath from the front door was a thick green curtain. This job was so successful he decided to take out the range in the front room. This also went well apart from he made the fire surround, plastered it, and then painted it pink, which did not go too well with the dark green and cream (Southdown Bus) paint acquired from a friend which the front room was painted in. He was a trier bless him!

He had his own business sub-contracting ceiling fixing and at one stage he had five or six men working for him. I worked for him for a couple of years; there are a few interesting stories about this time but I will save them for later.

Back to growing up. My eldest brother, Frank, was too grown up to be that interested in me. I remember he was in the Merchant Navy and we could not wait for him to come home on leave. He had a good job as a Head Bar Steward on the big liners. When he came home he would bring home stuff we rarely saw like an arm of bananas or large tins of salted peanuts, tins of sweets and pineapples. He used to travel to America, Australia and the Tropics. He came home one day and said he had had enough, stayed a week then promptly joined the Army! I never did understand why he was one of those people if he had something he had to find out how it worked. This particular day he had this wind up gramophone in pieces. The regulator was three lead weights which spun around at high speed, well this flew apart – one went through the window, one hit Colin between the eyes almost laying him out and the other we never did find!

Another time we had this Triumph motorcycle (would be a classic today!) and it had a sprung back hub. This had hundreds of springs in it, and he got in such a state trying to put it back together you could not talk to him. Anyway he had to take it to the garage to get it fixed.

At one time he owned a Bond three-wheeler. Well he turned this over going too fast and the roof cracked apart like an egg. Anyone else would have got rid, not Frank. He drilled small holes all along the sides of the car and laced it up with strong fishing line and fibreglassed it over the top. It looked like it had a huge egg.

My brother, Colin, and I were not that close as kids and went our own ways but when we got older we got very close as we are now. I remember we went over to the tip and found an old tandem one day. We took it back home and got it working. We took it to the slope that runs down to the canal basin. We met up with another four mates. All six of us piled on it and went down the hill. Well at the bottom we hit a pothole, the front wheel collapsed and we all went over the top, cuts and bruises but no real damage!

Very close to there was where they unloaded the gravel off the ships, there was a huge great pile of gravel which we used to climb. We had a sheet of corrugated iron which we slid down like a sledge. This particular day one of the lads (Tomy Bodden) climbed to the top and slipped backwards. He slid down the other side and straight into the canal. We all scrambled down and pulled him out, lucky he could swim!

Tomy and I were out one day and I kicked a discarded fag packet and out fell a pound note. We were rich, what would we do with it? I don't know why but we decided to run away to London. I suppose we had heard about the bright lights. We bought two tickets and off we went, our pockets full of sweets and chocolate bars. When we got there we had no idea where to go so we walked and walked for what seemed like miles. We saw absolutely nothing but houses and flats, no bright lights. We found this big park and sat in these bushes scoffing our sweets. It started to rain and after an hour we were feeling very wet and very sick. We then went and found a policeman who took us to the

Police Station. After a few hours we were put in a police car and taken back to Brighton. We were met by our two dads and got home and had a good hiding. I never saw Tomy again after that!

This part of the story you might find a bit boring. At five and a half we would walk to school in our short grey trousers and heavy black shoes and thick socks which had to be pulled up every other minute. Our shoes often got holes in them and so we used a folded up cigarette packet and put it inside to cover the hole. In the rain it was wellies which rubbed the backs of your legs sore. My father used to buy leather for the soles and rubber heels and mend our shoes which was common practice in those days.

I think I should explain to you what our house was like. Our front door opened on to the main road, and the threshold was so worn you could crouch down and see peoples' feet the other side. You went down two steps into the scullery which had a cobbled floor. This was about eight feet by five and had a butler sink, an oven, and a copper for washing your clothes and the like. There was a badly fitted back door which led into the yard. This also was cobbled. Up the far end was an outside toilet. It had an overhead cistern with chain. The seat was bleached and scrubbed white. There was a hook on the wall for toilet paper (newspaper torn into squares), the door had a nine inch gap top and bottom, it was always full of spiders. Also in the yard was a mangle for squeezing water out of the washing.

In the front room up above the window was a speaker down by the wall was the switch. You could get BBC, the

Home and the Light programs. We were supposed to pay for this but they installed it and forgot we had it so there was always music in our lives. We would listen to programs like Uncle Mac's, Children's Requests, Billy Cotton Band Show, the Goon Show, Hancock's Half Hour, The Third Man, Desert Island Discs and of course Dick Barton Special Agent. If you were out in the street playing and you heard the music the street would empty. My father would listen to the boxing matches and the football. As kids we would sneak down and sit on the top of the stairs to listen.

I mentioned the house was dark and dingy, this was because it wasn't too far from the gasworks and power station and they used to belch out smoke and soot all day. If the wind blew from the south everything ended up black. The doors and sash windows did not fit too well and rattled in the wind also letting the soot in. The winters were particularly hard, we had no central heating. We often scraped the ice off the inside of the windows. We piled coats on our beds to keep warm.

My job, being the youngest, first thing in the morning come rain or snow was to get the pee pots, take them downstairs and out into the yard, up to the toilet and empty them. Not much fun. The other job I disliked was to have to peel the potatoes before I went to school for the evening meal.

School days, being a small kid with ginger hair, I got picked on quite a bit. I used to try and make a joke of everything but this did not go down too good with the teachers. I had the cane quite often and the odd ruler broken on my hand. We had one teacher who used to make you bend over and give you a whack with a size ten slipper! I remember in a lesson not quite understanding what was happening, asking a question and getting a slap around the ear instead of getting an explanation! If you spoke in class you had to duck a piece of chalk or the blackboard rubber. Although being athletic later in life, at school I did not like sport, I suppose because I was so small. I came last in everything.

CHAPTER TWO

Around the time when I was ten or eleven was when I had my first brush with death. It started towards the end of my August holidays. I started to feel sick. I did not take much notice of it. I had stomach pains and started throwing up. I still went back to school at Portslade Secondary Modern. We had no playing field and we all had to traipse up to the girls' school, best part of a mile. Well this particular day we arrived at the playing field and were told we were going to play rugby. None of us knew anything about the game when this sixteen stone teacher ran through the rules none of us had a clue. Eventually I got the ball and I ran. The next thing I remember was a very large teacher diving on my back. The pointed end of the ball went into my stomach, I felt like it had come out my back. There was a terrible pain, the teacher realised there was something wrong, then put me on the crossbar of his bike and raced me down to Hove General Hospital (sadly no longer there). It turned out I had a burst appendix (peritonitis) – life threatening. Anyway I was in there for about a month and made a full recovery. The best bit was I had a month off school.

This walk up to the girls' school was quite interesting. Before Vale Road was built it was all part of Broomfield's Farm and we were left to our own devices to get home. I remember watching one of the farmers taking down a haystack. He was circling the stack with his walking stick. He could see something I could not, every now and again he would flick his stick and out would fall a dead mouse with a broken neck. It was amazing to watch.

Also when they pulled the carrots they used to put them in a very big circular bin filled with water and they would wash them with big bass brooms, we always ended up with a large carrot to munch all the way home.

There were several ways home from Mile Oak School, one way was through the allotments and of course we were always hungry so there were apples to scrump and strawberries. One memory was laying on my back between blackcurrant bushes eating bunches of these; scrumping apples was carried out like a military operation, we had look outs that could whistle very loud with three fingers. Learning how to do this was very difficult. If you heard the whistle you ran often through loads of stinging nettles with short trousers. It could be very painful!

In the holidays we were very lucky, not far away to the south was the canal, lagoon, or beach. To the North was the golf course and the downs. We didn't seem to play in parks, they seemed quite boring. To the side of the Golf Course there was a wood with a winding path, plenty of hideaways and camps. There were chestnut trees and beech trees, plenty more to eat, even blackberries. We also collected stray golf balls which we would take to the golf club and get a few coppers for them. We used to make catapults and try to shoot rabbits and birds – never hit a thing!

As I got older and bigger I occasionally went to work with my dad. I can remember him striding out and me trying to keep up with him. He carried the lunch boxes and a large bag of nails. The old fella shouting at me to hurry up or we would miss the train. When I actually started working for him I got paid one halfpenny per yard for fixing ceilings. As I got older it increased to one penny. I worked days and sometimes weekends.

One time my dad said there was a bungalow in Benfield Way, Portslade, and I had to go and sort it out. I walked up there with the tools (hammer, knife and nails) in a bag. I found this place and found it was all closed up so I got in through a window. I started work and within twenty minutes there were blue flashing lights and coppers everywhere; apparently someone had seen me go in through the window. It took me ages to explain but in the end they let me carry on. The thing is I looked very young to be working on my own.

By this time my father had found a new lady. At first she was quite nice but thing soon changed. We boys just did not hit it off with her, there were many rows ending up with violence. I remember severe strappings. She would pick up anything and hit us with it and I remember a broom being broken over my back. As I say we were quite a handful so we probably deserved it.

Christmas at North Street was amazing. We always had a real tree (no artificial ones in those days!). We made our own decorations and I think most people saved up money in several Christmas clubs. One in the butcher's, one in the grocer's and the other of course in the pub. Therefore, there was always plenty to eat and drink. In those days we had a large sideboard which was covered in fruit and sweets and in the middle there was a small barrel of beer. There was wine, bottles of cherryade, lemonade, Tizer, figs, dates, Turkish delights, tins of Quality Street, stuff we never saw until Christmas. There was holly and mistletoe. The tree had real candles on which were lit on Christmas Day evening. We sang carols, played games and ate until we felt sick! Christmas dinner was a banquet.

We would wake up very early and find our sock which we had put out on Christmas Eve. It would have an apple, an orange, a banana, some sweets, pencils, a colouring book and a toy. One time I had a little clown that was suspended between two sticks. When you squeezed the sticks together at the bottom the clown would jump and dance. I remember Colin was very jealous. When we heard some movement in our parents' room we would go in with their presents. The same old things every year. For my stepmum (Jean) a pot of Ponds Cold Cream and for Dad a packet of fags all wrapped up in Christmas paper. We would then get up, clean out the old ashes and light the fire. I think that was the only time we had a cooked breakfast otherwise it was cornflakes or porridge.

We never had many presents as things were tight. We understood and did not expect much. One time I got some roller skates which you strapped to your shoes. I think I nearly broke my neck on several occasions but I cracked it in the end and got quite good. Yes, Christmas was a magic time.

At one time my father was working up country and he came home with this big box. There was a strange noise coming from it. Well he put it on the floor, opened it up and inside was an incubator, a big metal circle with a small paraffin heater in the middle. Inside this were one hundred day old chicks. When they were old enough they were released into the yard. Somehow he managed to raise most of them, which he sold for Christmas. I remember trying to get past them to go to the outside loo. If the back door was not shut properly you would find them in the house. I think one even got upstairs; it was a mad house until they went. They were killed and sold for Christmas.

On a Saturday if I finished doing my chores and I could get sixpence together I would walk up Station Road to the Rothbury Cinema House which was quite new for Saturday morning pictures and you met a few mates and would watch short films. Things like westerns, Roy Rogers, Buck Rogers and the Lone Ranger and Tonto. There was the odd cartoon and silent comedy film but generally it was Laurel and Hardy, Abbott and Lou Costello and The Three Stooges. I might mention all American then the Pathé Pictorial would come on and finally the Queen with the National Anthem. Then it was a mass exit; that's where the saying came from 'get out before the Queen comes on'. Later in time came Tarzan of The Jungle and Flash Gordon Saviour of the Universe.

In those days we had several callers come to the front door. There was the insurance man, the man from the Provident and the Tally Man. You would order clothes and shoes from him and pay him so much a week. He was a lovely Jewish person and we struck up a friendship. He and I would go fishing quite a lot and chat for hours. One thing he said has stuck in my mind for all these years and it came true. He said, "One day Britain will become completely Americanised."

CHAPTER THREE

After I left home, I used to spend many afternoons chatting to my stepmother; funny how people change! Anyway back to growing up. Starting work with my father I think got me ready for life in general with lots of laughs and lots of pain. Because we were sub contractors we used to go on many sites for many different builders all over Sussex. This particular day we went to a site of bungalows in Lancing. I was about sixteen at the time. I had given this spred (plasterer) too much backchat when he flicked a bit of plaster at me which hit me in the back of the head so I retaliated by throwing a handful of nails which I had in my pouch at his newly plastered wall. He was not amused and chased me, caught me, marched me out the front – there his labourer had just mixed a new gauge of cement. He bent me over and stuck my head right in it, it was in my hair, ears, eyes, nose and mouth. I had to stagger to the standpipe and stick my head underneath. This was in the winter, I was cold and wet. It made me realise that arguing with the wrong person was definitely not on!

There were no O Levels or GCSEs in our day, therefore, everything I learned was from asking questions and watching really skilled men; no women on site in those days. I don't think people realise how hard the building site was, cement was all mixed up by hand, there were no site lifts, everything had to be carried by hand.

I taught myself many jobs. I was first and foremost a plasterboard fixer. I then learned how to plaster, artex ceilings, dry lining, decorating including wallpaper hanging, carpentry and the hardest job of all – roof tiling. I say this because you were out in all weathers. I remember having to sweep the snow off the felt before fixing the tiles. Nowadays they have machines to do jobs but back then it was all done by hand. On your head you wore a beret, or a back to front cap. In this we had a padded ring, we sorted out about eight tiles in a stack, swung these up on your head which you balanced. You then walked to the ladder, sometimes three storeys high! You climbed and when you got to the top you then had to climb the roof, you put them into rows (called cants) then of course they had to be fixed. We never climbed down ladders we put our hands and feet on the outside of the pole ladder and slid down. The bundle of tile battens was heavy and even heavier when soaked.

The fella I worked with, Keith, would run and make me run all day. I remember working in shorts when there was snow on the ground. In the summer it had its perks. The women watched and the girls would wolf whistle. Keith and I would be the best of friends. He died recently (2012).

All the years I did it I never went through a roof or fell off, many did. Roofing was a hard job, back to the days of being a ceiling fixer I would like to add in those days there was no such thing as health and safety! I have seen things that would make your hair curl. I have worked on scaffold over three storeys high with no hand rails and no kick boards. There were no hi viz jackets, steel toe caps or hard hats.

This is a little hard to explain so bear with me and I will try. When we were doing ceilings we worked off an eight foot scaffold board supported each end by a carpenter's trestle. We then carried the plasterboard to the scaffold and simultaneously swung it over our heads. This weighed over half a hundred weight. We would support this with just one hand and nail it into the joists with the other. There was a knack to this. You could get very fast, which meant more work and more money. Sometimes one got careless and frequently someone would step on a piece of discarded tile batten with a nail in it, quite painful. Another thing that often occurred was when you were cutting plasterboards you often slipped and sliced your fingers. There were also a few black fingers and thumbs. When you got really good you could slice boards up and fix them on your own. As I might have said before I got very fit, this helped me later in life as you will find out.

Something Health and Safety would have had a field day about may be hard to explain. When fixing ceilings in some houses there were no stairs so to get upstairs there was often a short pole ladder. If not, we would put a scaffold board up and climb up that, but if we couldn't reach the ceiling we would improvise. First we put a trestle on the edge of the place where the stairs should have been. We would then put the other trestle as far away as possible with a long scaffold board across the two trestles overhanging the well hole. A bit like a pirate's plank. The heaviest would sit on one end and the other would walk the plank and fix the ceiling. We would also work off five five-gallon cans which were very wobbly. There were many falls. Accidents happened all the time, it was the way things were. We also had many laughs.

My father bought this Fordson Van, green it was, a right pile of junk. The steering wheel was so stiff you had to force it round, the wipers worked by vacuum and when you came to a hill they slowed down to a standstill. It drank oil and belched out blue smoke. We were coming home from work one day, going through Worthing when there was this huge bang and this hole appeared in the bonnet. We stopped immediately, got out to open the bonnet and this policeman came up to us and said, "'Does this belong to you?" and handed us a blade off the cooling fan. They were made of metal in those days. It had completely broken apart, this blade had hit the road and ricocheted just past this copper's ear! One had gone with such a force it had gone straight through the bonnet, we never did find the other two.

Another time we were going through Hove when all of a sudden the front of the van dipped one side and came to an abrupt halt. The wheel had come off and was heading at a rate of knots towards the shop windows. It hit between the windows luckily for us!

I remember one day coming home from Horsham we ran out of petrol. In Hangleton by the windmill there were four of us in it at the time. Well we all got out and started pushing. We got it rolling and two jumped back inside. The driver and I opened the door got half in and started scooting. We got to Hangleton Road and jumped back in. We were free wheeling down the hill to the traffic lights. They were red so we slowed down and they turned to green. We started scooting again down to the railway crossing in Portslade. The man who was up in the box winding the handle was closing the gates, as we approached. We yelled up to him and he opened the gates enough for us to squeeze through. We carried on scooting down Station Road to North Street where I lived. We were absolutely knackered – you must remember the volume of traffic was nothing compared to today.

We had several vans after that but none as bad as that one. One evening when I was a lad some mates and I pushed it from outside my house about fifty yards so it could not be heard starting up (you could start it with a screwdriver). I was only fifteen but I drove them up to Steyning and Bramber and back. The next morning the old man could not figure out where the petrol had gone, he thought it had a petrol leak. I even learned how to drive by watching people.

Another evening one of my mates, Colin Jenner as I remember, said, "I've got my dad's keys and his car is in the car park of the pub." So off we went to the car park. I was the only one who could drive so it was down to me. We all piled in. What I did not realise was it was a Ford Consul and it had the gear lever on the steering column. I had never even seen one before! Well it was parked in front of a two foot high wall. I started it up, pushed in the clutch, put it in gear, after an effort let out the clutch and it snatched. Well, I was not in reverse as I thought. We shot forward demolishing the wall and leaving the front wheels overhanging the pavement and two feet off the ground. No need to say we all got out and ran! It was amazing nobody heard or saw a thing. I saw Colin the next day and he said his father had said he must have been pissed when he parked it the night before!

Let's talk about the cinemas or picture houses as they were called. There was the Pavilion, The Rothbury and later there was the Granada. The Pavilion was at the bottom of North Street. It was a right dive. I know they are supposed to be dark but this place was blacker than night. When you went in you were shown to your seat. Well you had to find one without a spring poking through! The gents' toilets were foul and when the door opened this foul smell would waft through the place. There was a piano up the front left over from the silent movies. In the middle of a film someone would sneak up the centre aisle and play a few bars. Sometimes the film would break and a big cheer would go up. Sometimes the Projectionist would get it wrong and the picture was wider than the screen so the Goodies were shooting from the gents' and the baddies from the ladies' to a huge applause. Also someone would often dangle a scarf from the balcony in front of the projector. In the gents' there was a fire exit, well we often went in the toilet and let in half a dozen of our mates. Eventually it got so bad it closed down.

Outside where we lived the Salvation Army Brass Band would gather to sing and play, usually on a Sunday evening. Well when they started especially the bass drum everything in the house would rattle. Well in the dark winter evenings it was not too bad because after a little while Colin would go into the yard and pop out the streetlight with his air rifle. One particular evening my father was trying to listen to a football match on the radio and he suddenly snapped. He went to the front door and in no uncertain terms told them to f*** off! I must admit they never came back again!

Telling that story I just remember larking about with Colin and he accidently shot me with his air rifle. As luck would have it, it smashed my fly button to pieces. The pain was incredible and I still cringe when I think about it now.

As we got older we got more adventurous. We would pretend to go to bed early, climb out the bedroom window onto a low roof and go to the funfair. One night we stayed out until late, the old man caught us climbing back in the window. I think we felt his belt on our backsides for that. I keep jumping from one subject to another but I am writing these things down as I recall them, but all these things happened before I was fifteen.

We got allocated a new council house when I was about sixteen. It was in Thornhill Rise, Upper Portslade. It had a back garden with real grass, yippee! It also had a large grassed area at the front which came in very handy.

My eldest brother Frank, now there was a character. I can still see him two months stubble, ginger hair, riding his motorbike, a white peaked crash helmet and his great coat flapping in the wind. I went fishing off the Banjo Groyne in Hove often as he lived near there in a top floor flat, where I lived with him and his wife, Betty, for a while. I remember I came home one evening and he had been to the river at Shoreham and collected some mussels. Well he cooked them and asked me if I would like some. I didn't like mussels so I said, "No." Next day he was covered in big red blotches, he had food poisoning.

Another time he used to keep budgerigars and finches. We built an aviary up on the flat roof of the flat, quite a big thing. It was secured to the chimneys. He had about forty birds.

On this particular morning I said to him, "Did you hear that wind last night?"

"No," he said. "Slept through it," it was blowing a hooly. Well sheepishly we went up on the roof and it and the birds had gone, we looked all around but it had vanished, never to be seen again!

He loved pinball machines and lost a few bob on them. Later in life he got a job working on a farm. He loved this and I used to visit him with my second wife, a nice trip out to Polegate, on a Sunday afternoon. However, one morning I got a phone call, the lady on the other end informed me he had had a fatal accident. I was so shocked I asked how bad, apparently the farmer's horse had got out; he saw it and had gone to get it. It had reared up and kicked him in the head, killed him instantly, that was the end of poor Frank.

CHAPTER FOUR

When I left school at fifteen I turned from a snotty nose little kid into Jack the Lad. I was earning good money, more than most of my friends. I was buying my own clothes and fags, every youngster then emulated the film stars of the day, almost everybody in those days smoked. My father was no exception – sixty Captain full strength a day. I had seen him working on a scaffold with a fag in his mouth. It would burn down to nothing and he would spit it out and it would burn up as it floated to the floor. I have also seen him fall asleep in his armchair with a fag on. It would burn right down until it got to his lips, and go out, with one complete ash.

Anyway back to the plot. As I say when I reached fifteen I learned about sex, rock and roll, violence and adrenaline, but not in that order. I think the adrenaline came to the forefront when my brother came to visit. He would park his motorbike outside the house and I used to sit on it under the pretence of looking after it. It was a big bike, a Sunbeam as I remember. Well one day I started it up and inevitably started moving a little, and one day off I went. I went a few feet and rolled it back. I got braver and eventually went around the block. I got quicker and quicker and the buzz I got from this was amazing. Of course I had no licence or insurance, it was not illegal to wear a crash helmet but it did not bother me. This eventually led to a life of bikes and cars. I must admit I got a kick out of going fast and in the right place and time I still do. The violence I encountered was a jealous boyfriend – I will explain later.

The sex, well I will try and explain. In the evenings I would frequent this café. It was the beginning of the coffee bar era. We talked the owner into getting a juke box in the backroom and drank coffee. I remember it cost threepence to play a record; there was Elvis, Jerry Lee Lewis, Bill Haley, Little Richard and Pat Boon. That's where I learned to jive. Well this girl would come in now and again. She was a lot older than the rest of us, quite attractive but I think she put her make-up on with a trowel. She did not look too bad in the dim lights. Anyway I started chatting to her and she suggested we went outside. Well it was winter time and very dark. There was an alleyway next to the café and we went into it. Well she gave me a kiss and I closed my eyes like they do on the movies. I could not believe what happened next, she dropped down to her knees and undid my fly. I can't say I did not enjoy it but when I opened my eyes eventually she was gone. I tidied myself up and went back into the café to a barrage of questions from my mates. I was too dazed to answer them, I just sat there with a glazed expression on my face in pure disbelief. We were told later she was on the game, but to this day I never knew if she was a girl or a bloke!

At this time most of us lads went into Brighton and had our suits made. We went to Samy Gordons, you picked the material and the style, and picked it up the following week. It cost about seven pounds ten shillings. We really thought we were the bees knees. Our long jackets with the velvet collars, our drainpipe trousers and our thick crepe soles (brothel creepers) suede shoes. We also had the obligatory Tony Curtis hair cut. He was a famous film star at that time.

The tax man and the National Insurance men were always chasing me as they did most of the lads so I thought I would get a proper job, something with prospects. In the meantime I had passed my driving test amazingly. In those days you still had to give hand signals. Well I came up to this corner and the test fella said turn right. I was changing down a gear with my left hand and stuck my right hand out the window to do the hand signal. Well of course I had no hands on the steering wheel. He grabbed the wheel and told me to pull in. I thought that was me finished but after a rollicking he said I had passed.

Building in those days were hard, the fella who owned the café, Ted, also worked on a ship as a cook. This was a smallish tanker which came into Shoreham, in fact it unloaded just down the road at the Oil Depot. Well he told me they needed a Deckhand. The idea of joining the Merchant Navy and seeing the world (like my brother, Frank) appealed to me greatly, little did I know. I went down to where the ship was moored, saw the skipper and got the job. I went home and told my parents who were not too happy. Anyway I had made up my mind. I stuffed some gear in my bag and off I went. I hadn't felt like this before, I felt all shaky and nervous. I was introduced to the crew, the skipper, the mate, the able seaman, the chief engineer and of course the cook, who I already knew. I was told my rank was an ordinary seaman and I was shown everything and what it was for, the binnacle compass which told you your direction, a round thing supported by a post with a handle which sent instructions to the engine room. It was very basic. There was a large ship's wheel, it was as tall as my chest. It was polished wood and brass. In fact most things were made of brass. I know it was one of my jobs to polish it.

Where do I start? I suppose I started as a general dogsbody. My day started usually very fast. The first job was to start up the generator which put all the lights on, the jenny, as we called it, was a diesel engine which had to be started by swinging this big handle. Then I had to light the fire in the galley which was at the stern of the ship (This is hard to believe a coal fire on an oil tanker!) First I had to get some coal, sounds easy. First get a bucket, take it to the hatch of the hold in which we stored most things; rope, paint, bits and pieces and coal. I would open the hatch, above this was a pulley and rope with a hook on the end. I would lower the bucket into the bottom and fill it with coal. I would then climb back up the ladder and carry it to the galley. If the sea was a bit rough this could be quite a job as the bucket would usually end up half empty.

A couple of names stick in my mind; dhoby and soogee. Dhoby was washing your clothes and soogee was to wash the white paint on the side of the ship. That was a lousy job. Sometimes you had to hang precariously over the side of the ship on a couple of rope ladders to achieve this! It was a weird sort of job because you never got a proper night's sleep. You sailed when the tide was right so it could be anytime of the day or night. When we were on the quay at Southampton or Poole it was a tidal mooring so it had a large rise and fall. Well this meant you had to keep getting up every hour to loosen or tighten the ropes. Sometimes you would doze off, and would be abruptly woken by the bang bang bang. It was the ropes stretching to their limits. You would rush out of the Folksall, where you had your bunk, and find the ship virtually hanging on the ropes. A couple of these were steel cables; we called them Springs. When you slackened them off they would slide through your hands and they would have broken strands which would tear your hands to bits.

Some mornings there would be snow or heavy frost. If you didn't have gloves on your hands would stick to the metal of the ship.

Another job which was bad news and very dangerous was to wash the tanks out. The oil we carried was gas oil (diesel) and Britolium which was very thick black oil. The britt would stick to the side of the tanks, therefore, they had to be washed down. First of all I had to put on a rubber suit with a hood, rubber wellies, a pair of goggles (no mask) and rubber gloves. Next you would lower the pressure gun into the tank. This was like a fireman's hose but half the size. You would then climb down a metal ladder that was coated in thick black oil. At the bottom you wedged yourself into a corner as best you could, grabbed the hose gun, signalled to whoever was at the hatch to turn on the pumps, you then crossed your fingers and pulled the trigger. The noise of the pumps rattled around the tank, it was horrendous! In the corner there was a large hole which sucked the old mixture of britt and diesel waste as you were washing it down with diesel. This was then pumped into a tank to be disposed of later. Yes it was quite an experience.

The engine room was kept spotless by the chief engineer. The paintwork was like new and the pipes and levers were gleaming, very highly polished. There were three generators, pumps, dials and of course the engine. It was huge, a four cylinder diesel, twelve feet long and it ran so slow you could hear the cylinders fire in order. I saw it stripped down once and the pistons were like dustbins. There wasn't an oily rag in sight.

The Fo'c'isle was at the topside bow of the ship. This is where two of us stayed, the able seaman and myself. There were two bunks, a small coal fire, a lamp on gimbles and a couple of lockers. There was also a small wash basin which had no S bend because the waste water ran straight into the sea. When it was rough the sea water was flushed back up the plughole like a fountain and the floor was swimming in water. Also in the Folksall there was a big iron ducting which the anchor chain ran in. When it was rough this crashed and rattled and the noise was deafening. The bow of the boat would come out of the water and crash back down, and sometimes you would even leave your bunk.

Somehow you would have to try and sleep through this, often cold and damp.

There was also many good times and lots of laughs. First I must tell you about this mad Irishman who joined the ship as an able seaman. Well a few years earlier I had learned to scull a boat. This was propelling the dingy forward by twisting a single oar from side to side while standing up. Well Paddy hadn't seen this before. I told him I would show him how to do it. Later this particular night we were moored up to a buoy because our berth was taken up with another ship. The skipper and crew had gone ashore and I was left on watch.

Earlier that day I had caught a bucket full of mackerel and left them in the galley. There was nothing to do and so I had an early night. When I woke in the morning there was mud everywhere and the galley was in one hell of a mess. Apparently Paddy had come back to the ship well bladdered. He had tried to scull the jolly boat, got in a mess and had ended up on one of the mud flats. He had to be rescued by the Coastguard and they brought him back to the ship. He came aboard and went to the galley where he cooked all the fish and ate them all. In the morning when he surfaced he got the biggest bollocking and was close to getting the sack.

This Irishman was a big guy, as hard as nails and as strong as an ox. The reason for saying this is because what happened next would probably have killed a normal person. Well we were coming back from Southampton, it was a foul night, raining and blowing gale force winds. As she was a tanker she sat very low in the water and the waves were breaking over the bow, rolling along the deck, hitting the pump house and breaking over the wheelhouse. When we got to Shoreham the tide was too low to get in the harbour so we had to anchor off and wait for the tide. I think that was the first and only time I have ever felt seasick. After a couple of hours the skipper said we were going in so Paddy, myself and the mate went to the anchor winch on the bow. The weather had abated a little but the odd wave came over the front almost knocking you off your feet. We had to raise the anchor by winding a large handle either side of the winch. Paddy grabbed one handle and I took the other.

"Take the strain," the mate shouted and released the brake. Well just then the ship's bow dropped and rose on a wave, the force of the anchor ripped the handles out of our hands. I jumped back but Paddy was a bit slower and the spinning handle hit him straight across the forehead, He fell backwards and when we looked his whole forehead had dropped leaving a huge gash. There was claret everywhere, we got him back to the galley and laid him down and all he wanted was a fag. When we docked the ambulance was there to meet us and then took him away. One week later we had been to Southampton and back, we pulled into the dock and there he stood, large as life a big grin on his face and a very impressive row of stitches like the Frankenstein monster. Just after this he left the ship.

I remember one day going down to the engine room and in the middle of the floor stood this tatty old cement mixer. Apparently they had nicked it the night before off the dock.

After a week the Chief Engineer had transformed it into a gleaming new machine which was promptly sold. Sometimes we were in port for two or three days. If we were in Southampton the Cook would drive me back to Portslade for a day. He had this old Bedford van in which he had two five gallon jerry cans. On the quay there were large pipes which took all the oil and fuel to the tanks, all these pipes had small drain taps and at night we would get on the quay and drain off petrol for the van. When we went home the following day the van went like a bat out of hell. Well apparently we had gone to the wrong pipe and filled it with high octain aircraft fuel and two miles from Worthing the engine blew up.

Back on the ship there were some very good times and some horrendous times. We had a lot of laughs when I was learning to steer the ship and read the compass. It took us twice as long to get anywhere. The wake was zig zag all the way down the channel. In the end I soon got the hang of it and got quite competent. I must mention the skipper and the mate were both pissheads and would often go to their cabins telling us some excuse but we all knew why. As soon as we left the harbour out would come the excuse. They would say, "You know the co-ordinates, Brian, I'm going to get my head down for a bit." There I was, a seventeen year old kid in charge of a three hundred ton oil tanker! I loved it. It made me feel great.

Often we would pass a ship coming the other way and we would pass quite close. I would open the wheelhouse door and wave or shout to them. When we got to

Southampton I would go and wake the skipper and he would take the ship in.

We would often do bunkering which was loading fuel onto other big ships and to do this was quite an art as you had to regulate which valves to open and shut. This was done by turning large wheels. It was quite primitive. Occasionally we would run down to the river Hamble and we would pass the Woolston chain ferry; this was another antique. The river at low tide ran down at about seven knots. Well our ship only did seven knots and when we got to the ferry the ship would come to a standstill and we would have to wait until the tide came up before we would make any headway.

In the winter we would often get thick fog. This was quite a scary event because we had no radar. My job was to stand up on the bow and look and listen. I would then shout back to the skipper who was in the wheelhouse which was behind us. There were loads of obstacles in Southampton water; there were the forts, buoys, long metal stakes and of course the odd ship. We would go very slowly. We would run the engine for five minutes, then stop for five and listen. The buoys were not too bad, they usually had a bell. As they came out of the fog they were huge and always gave me a fright! In the summer it was so busy we would often collide with a couple of small yachts. I think they expected us to get out of the way as there was an unwritten law which said motors give way to sails but our manoeuvrability was very limited.

I have just remembered a situation I got myself into when we were berthed at Shoreham. Everyone had shot off home and left me to discharge the tanks, something I had done many times before. I had connected the hoses, started up the pumps and opened the valves. I knew it would take a couple of hours to unload and so I went ashore and nipped up the road to the café. I started nattering and drinking tea. After an hour and a half I thought I had better get back to the ship. I took a stroll back and got to the steps. I looked down at the ship and had the shock of my life… the ship was listing to port at a very nasty angle. In fact the gunwhale was underwater. I rushed down and opened the port valves and closed the starboard ones, and slowly she levelled up. It was a very close call!

I had just passed my exams and was about to pick up my seaman's ticket when it all happened. It was a lovely summer's day and we were going back to Shoreham. We had just come through the lock gates and were heading down to our berth. I was sorting out the rope when the skipper shouted from the wheelhouse, "Brian, there are no huffers to get the ropes."

What he did was very slowly nose the boat into the quay and I would jump ashore and take the mooring ropes. I had done it dozens of times before. Well this time I slipped and I fell between the ship and the quay. I remember coming to the surface and trying to push the ship away. I may have been a strong lad but trying to stop two hundred and fifty tons was asking a bit much. After that everything got a bit hazy. The ship rolled me along the quay like a fender. I remember seeing five gallon drums in the same place being squashed flat. Anyway I did not pass out and I remember them pulling me out (because it was a tanker the gunwhales were very low). They laid me on the deck, my legs were facing the deck and I was facing the sky. I asked them to straighten me out which obviously they could not. I remember going in the ambulance to Hove Hospital. They stuck a needle in my arm and I woke two days later in the Sussex County Hospital in Brighton. I was paralysed from the waist down.

They told my family I would never walk again, quite a shock for them and me as a teenager. Apparently I was very lucky; the piles at the quay run vertically but where we moored there was one running horizontally. This was just below the water. If it had been the other way my chest and ribs would have been crushed and I would not be writing this now. Instead I had a crushed pelvis, bladder and double rupture. I was in intensive care for a few weeks and then moved to Valance Ward.

In those days hospitals were very different than today. The Matron, who was in charge, ran the place with a rod of iron. It was very military. She would come down to the ward every Monday and do an inspection. Everything had to be spick and span with nothing out of place. Even the beds had to be made with special envelope folds. If there was a spot of dust someone was for the high jump. I had a lovely twelve inch scar and pipes going in and coming out everywhere. I had one pipe in my stomach attached to a machine under my bed which was literally taking the piss!

There was a lot of pain and tears at first but a few months on things got much better. In the middle of the ward there was a piano and on Sundays the Salvation Army would come and expect you to sing hymns. Believe me when you were laying there in pain that was the last thing you needed! Had visits from my mates. I still smile when I think back to the clothes they wore. A very large check drape jacket with a velvet collar, elasticated tight light blue trousers and thick crepe soled brothel creepers. With Tony Curtis haircuts they looked like a bunch of clowns. They would all bring me in a packet of fags or a bottle of beer. I hardly smoked at all so in the end I had a locker full of fags.

I had several other small operations and I got very used to the way things worked. If you wanted a boiled egg for breakfast you had to get someone to bring you in some and they would collect them, write your name on it and send it down to the kitchen. I got friendly with this feller who had a smallholding and his wife would bring in these duck eggs. After that I had duck eggs every morning. Colin, who was in the Army in Germany, was flown home on compassionate leave. I know he was not too pleased about that because he was counting down the days to his demob. Thanks to him I got walking again. I used to have physiotherapy every day but nothing moved below my waist.

My brother used to grab my feet and wiggle them at the same time he would swear at me. "Move your feet, you bastard."

Gradually the feeling came back and slowly I started to move my legs. They came down one morning and said, "We are going to get you up today."

I had been on my back for eight months and it was a bit of a shock! Anyway they fetched me a wheelchair and two physios sat me on the side of the bed. They then swung my legs around and they looked like matchsticks; the muscles had wasted away. They asked me to stand up, which I did. As I stood up straight the whole room went round and round and I awoke back on my bed with the doctor, nurses and physios. I was OK but I could sense they were concerned. Apparently I had passed out and hit the floor like a sack of spuds. Eventually I managed to transfer to a wheelchair that was much more enjoyable. I could get around and see people and chat. Because it was unique for a person to recover the way I did they liked to show me off to other doctors and trainee nurses. The first time this happened I was laying in bed starkers when this group of young girls and a doctor came over and whipped off my sheets. I don't know who was more embarrassed, them or me. In the end nothing ever bothered me, I had been pushed and proded so many times and exposed to everyone I didn't even take much notice. I remember talking to a male nurse one day while he was shaving me down below. I said to him, "What kind of a job is that?" He replied, "I know, after the first five times all the fun goes out of it."

We had this fella on the ward, he was ninety-four years old; everyone called him Pop Bonwick. He came from Whitehawk (a dodgy part of Brighton). He had dozens of visitors who came up and saw him. Lights out was at nine p.m. sharp. Everyone had settled down and there were a few snores when all hell broke loose. He had had a heart attack. The curtains were drawn very quickly and you could see all the shadows rushing around. Between ten p.m. and midnight he had four heart attacks. After they brought him round for the fourth time he settled down. They had remade his bed, got him a cup of tea, sorted out his catheter and as they stood back and asked if there was anything else they could get him, there was a short pause and then he replied, "Could you get me a good woman?"

The laughter around the ward erupted; everyone was awake.

When I got my wheelchair I also got a few jobs to do. I would run errands like deliver notes and things to other wards. In the evening I emptied bottles in the sluice, I also made the drinks for the patients. I would put the stuff on the trolley and the hot milk and I would ask them what they wanted; milk, Horlicks or Cocoa. Most of them wanted Horlicks. I put a spoonful of Horlicks in and then added the hot milk. They all said thanks and then drank it. Nobody said a word. When I finished I thought I would have one myself. I tasted it and it was foul! I had a close look at the Horlicks tin and there was a small piece of sticking plaster with 'mustard' written on it! I went into the kitchen and there was a row of Horlicks tins on the shelf. Everything was stored in empty Horlicks tins! I often wonder how many poor old souls I helped on their way.

As time went on I progressed to a pair of crutches, wooden ones. They were hard work and then one day someone turned up with a pair of aluminium ones. They clipped on my arms and I could get to a fair old speed on them.

I had been in there a whole year. I remember the day I came out; there was a lot of hand shaking, hugs and kisses and a few tears shed on both sides. It was the fourth July, American Independence Day. It felt very strange on the outside, I think it was Colin who picked me up. He had borrowed a car because all he had was a small Francis-Barnett motorcycle.

I soon got very good on my crutches and I could almost run with them. I would go from Mile Oak down to Portslade to the café every day, drink coffee and listen to the music on the jukebox, people like Elvis, Cliff, Little Richard, Jerry Lee Lewis. I preferred rock and roll to jazz and ballads. In fact, I learned to jive on my crutches. Those days were magic, that was the start of real rock and roll.

Because the café was used by the bus drivers and the general public we all changed to another, a place in North Street called Reo's. I soon discarded my crutches. I do remember while still on crutches on the way home late at night I would walk past a certain girl's house. She was a lovely girl, very free and easy. I had known her for years. As I got to her gate I would whistle; two minutes later her front door would open. We would kiss and cuddle and end up having a quickly on the stairs. I would then carry on home.

At one time I acquired an Austin Seven and it was parked outside on the waste ground in front of our house. It had no starter motor just a handle in the front which you had to swing. Well me and the lads painted it multi colours. I know the doors were painted yellow and had large skull and crossbones in black on them. I thought it looked great. When I got home from work in the evenings I tinkered with the engine and gave the handle a couple of swings. My dad said I was wasting my time and it would never start. I proved him wrong when one day it burst into life. It even surprised me. Blue smoke everywhere.

Well I fiddled more and got to know quite a bit about engines. It had no tax or insurance but one afternoon two of my mates and a girl got in it and we went up the road to the downs. We were poodling along up and down the hills quite nicely when my mate said, "Have you ever rolled a motor before?"

I said, "No, but I will have a go."

We were just going down a hill and I pulled the wheel hard over... over we went how many times we rolled I could not say but when we came to a halt there were arms and legs and bodies everywhere. When the dust settled to my amazement nobody was hurt, just a few bruises. We climbed out and the car was wrecked so we left it there and walked home.

About this time some of the lads started buying motorbikes and it was then the start of the Rockers began. We all got bigger and better bikes and it was the time of the leather jackets and denims influenced by James Dean and

Marlon Brando films. We would put our own studs in the jackets, there were no crash helmets in those days, and there were a few fatal accidents. One of the lads, Johny Mack, was going home one evening and the road men had left a trench with no barriers around it and he went straight down it. He died a few days later but we all thought 'it won't happen to me', No fear or no brains, who knows?

On Sunday mornings four or five of the lads would come up to my house and clean their bikes, they sparkled like new pins. After cleaning them we would then ride down to the café, I remember riding down there wearing a T-shirt, shorts and sandals, crazy when I think back. I had several bikes mainly Triumphs. There were Nortons BSAs, Royal Enfields and the odd Valocette. There were also Douglas Dragonfly iconic collectors' bikes.

In those days the coffee bars and cafes all had jukeboxes — Rock-Ola or Ball-amy's and the records were updated every week. I used to buy the old records off the fella and I had quite a collection.

There were also the pinball machines and of course we would also jive. I loved dancing and showing off my moves; the girls also loved it.

One day we went down the café and Reo was not there. His wife told us he was in hospital. Shortly after that the café shut down, alas no more Reo's. After that we moved down to Roko's Café down by Hove Lagoon, it was next to the Blue Anchor pub and so we all called it the Anchor Café. It was much better and there was a bigger variety of food. We also got to meet a lot of new friends from Hove.

One I still see once a week, we are very good mates, good old Alan.

My brother, Colin, had just got a job driving a JCB digger and he had a job that was local. One Saturday afternoon he turned up with it down at the café and the girls had a great time riding up and down the road in the front bucket. Another thing we used to do which I think we saw in a film, was to put a record on the jukebox and get on the bike and go around the block before the record stopped — three minutes! We also visited other cafes. There was Jamie's, The Green Turtle in Lancing and a place in Hurstpierpoint. Often on a Saturday afternoon eight or ten or us would drive to Brighton to the Princes News Cinema just down from the Clock Tower and we would watch an hour of cartoons, no one would sit in front of us because we would stand our leather jackets on the seat in front and put our crash helmets on top so it looked like someone was sitting there. Sometimes one of the lads would say he had an auntie in Dover or Weymouth, anywhere really, and we would all get on our bikes and go in a convoy. It was great because there were very few cars about then. We were coming home one day along the Kingsway in Hove, eight abreast and two deep, well we were stopped by this policeman. He stepped out with his hand up. We all stopped and he shouted, "I have never seen such an exhibition of driving in my life," to which one of the lads replied, "Well we are only learners." Even the copper smiled and told us to go.

We would often visit the different motorcycle shops, there was Tates and Portsglade Garages of Hove, Gray and Rousels was based in Shoreham, Redhill Motors of Brighton and the largest of all Pride and Clarke in Stockwell Road, London. Their shops were both sides of the whole street; they had hundreds of bikes. We would spend all day there.

We had plenty of spills. One day coming home, I was going around the bend in the Old Village. It was a bit damp and the back wheel hit a metal manhole; the bike went sideways and I slid along the road on my backside leaving a trail of sparks as in the back pocket of my jeans I had a tobacco tin. I came to a halt to a round of applause from the bus queue. I stood up and my arse was hanging out. I got back on my bike and rode home; no bruises but a very red face!

Another thing very vivid in my mind. My brother, Colin, had just bought a new Royal Enfield Constellation, a very fast bike in its day, quite capable of doing a ton. He asked me if I would like a ride, so I climbed on the pillion and off we went all through the country at breakneck speed. On the way home we were coming up King George V, which was also called Snakey Hill because it was extremely steep and bendy. My brother wanted to show me how quick the bike was so he opened up the throttle. We were doing about 80mph when up ahead there was a learner broadside across the road. As we started to go left she started to go forward so we swerved to the right and she started to go backwards. There was not any room to go back and I remember my brother saying, "Hang on." We mounted the kerb and went up the four foot grass bank at the side of the road, we were launched into space. I remember looking down and seeing people picnicking under us. We landed the bike on the waste ground. Colin drove to the exit and he stopped, I got off the bike and promptly threw up; that was something to tell the lads.

Later I bought myself a Triumph Speed Twin, it was black and white. It was quite a big bike and my brother told me it was too big for me. That evening I thought I would test it out and I went up the Devils Dyke. On the way back I went too fast around a bend and went straight through a barbed wire fence. I can still see the back light of the bike disappearing in the distance leaving me hanging on the fence. I went and retrieved the bike which didn't have a scratch on it; on the other hand my jeans were ripped and there was blood all over my legs. I rode home, cleaned myself up, changed my jeans and went back down the café. I never told a soul about that especially Colin. I still carry two scars on my thighs!

We often went to Brands Hatch and I remember deaf Dave breaking down and towing him back to Portslade with two bungee straps tied together. That was quite exciting.

Then along came the Mods with their scooters and parka coats with the furry collars. They had Vespers and Lambrettas covered in lights and horns, and plenty of chrome. The Mods and the Rockers did not get on, they had their café's and we had ours. There were plenty of fights, nothing serious just punch ups. Before the days of indicators on cars we had to learn hand signals, and then they fitted levers on the side of cars. They were illuminated and they were about five inches long. They would flick up and out. Well it was tempting not to bash them down when we overtook them. We also used our bikes to ride to work.

One morning we had this job in Bognor. It was absolutely pouring down, difficult to see when your goggles kept misting up. I had my mate Beck on the back at this time. We turned into the site and I saw this dead straight new concrete road. I got halfway down but the second half hadn't been laid, it was just a very level twelve inches of soft mud. With the heavy rain it looked like the road; we went straight off the end. I managed to keep the bike upright. I had mud up to my knees but poor old Beck fell straight in. I managed to get the bike into one of the bungalow's garages and got the hose. I hosed the bike down, then my legs and then poor old Beck. We were so cold and wet we just rode back home. Beck, his real name was Hector Macdonald Smith, we ribbed him about this (HMS) that's why he had us all calling him Beck. He was the brunt of many jokes.

I know I loved the motorbike days but what finished me was one day I was working in Crawley and I approached Bolney Steps. I was laying on the tank and had the bike full throttle flat out doing about a tonne when along the side of me pulled this Jaguar XK. He sat there smoking his pipe. He looked at me, shook his head, stuck his foot down and disappeared in the distance. After that episode I sold the bike and bought a van, not as quick but a lot more comfortable.

I had this mate, Derek Elliker, who worked for the General Post Office as a mechanic. He would work a lot at nights and I would drive up to Kemp Town and he would work on my car and after that I would keep him company. We would watch telly or play cards.

Well this particular evening he said, "Do you need anything doing?" I replied, "No." He said, "Well put your van through the car wash." I said, "OK," and drove it in, parked up and he started up the car wash. We then went to his Mess Room and we had a couple of bacon sandwiches and started watching TV. Well after about two hours he stood up and said, "That washer is still going."

We went out into the garage and it was still going; it would normally go up and down the vehicle twice and turn itself off. It had run up once and got stuck on the bumper of another van, the revolving brushes were stuck in one spot for two hours, it had taken the paintwork completely off down to the bare metal. After that I could not afford a repair so we painted it by hand, Post Office Yellow! All the lads and birds would pile in the back and go all over the place, it was not very comfortable so I decided to get a car.

Derek and I went to a car auction up at Frimley and I bought this Ford Cortina Estate. It was metallic green, mechanically it was sound but it had a hole in both wings but Derek said not to worry as they were bolted on. We changed the wings in about two hours and I did many miles in that car.

Another strange buy I had was a yellow Cortina GT. It had a black vinyl roof and I bought it with no wheels. I had seen it in the pub car park a couple of weeks earlier, it was up on bricks. Apparently the owner had drunk too much and left it overnight. When he went back in the morning he found it on four piles of bricks with the wheels missing. Well I traced him and made him a silly offer and he accepted. I went straight down the breakers yard and bought some sports wheels, fitted them, a nice cheap car – job done!

I have had too many cars to remember. I have bought some real bargains and some right old dogs. Apart from when I was in hospital I have driven a bike or a car almost every day since I was sixteen years old, that would be about fifty-five years. I have had one speeding fine and one accident, not bad. I also think I am privileged to have lived when I have, seeing the rock and roll days, the assassination of Martin Luther King, the assassination of President Kennedy, the rise of the Beatles, the IRA bombings in London, the shooting of John Lennon, the death of Princess Diana and even 9/11.

Anyway back to the job I got in this wine shop. They had several stores and made their own beer. I thought I might work my way up the ladder and get promotion. Well that never happened. I delivered wine, beer and spirits. I went to this block of flats with a couple of beers one day. It was tipping it down with rain. I had to use the fire escape around the back as it was the tradesman's entrance. Well I climbed to the top, knocked and waited; eventually this little old lady came to the door, so pleased to see me she asked me in and asked me if I could change a light bulb for her. I did this, she said thanks and down I traipsed. I was just getting back in the van when I heard this little voice call out to me. She beckoned me back; up I went, another climb up four flights. I got to her door and she gave me threepence tip. When I got back to the van I was soaked to my pants for threepence! Another time I went to some flats in the posh part of Hove. When they opened the door this fella was half naked; when I took the box in they were all naked or half naked dancing and singing. Well this fella who let me in asked me in a very feminine voice if I wanted to stay. I saw one fella get out his tool and piss in the middle of the floor. I made a very quick retreat from that one!

Most of these people had accounts with us and they would phone in their orders. One day it rung and it was one of our regulars, a Doctor Bulcock. It made me smile as he was always inebriated and it sounded like 'dropped a bollock'. He asked me to bring around a couple of bottles of Guinness which I did straight away. When I arrived he asked me in and asked me not to deliver anything to his wife. I said OK, so he bunged me a fiver and off I went. Later that afternoon his wife rang – could I bring around a half bottle of gin, so off I went. She was in the front room, bedridden so in I go very cautiously just in case.

When I gave her the gin, she said, 'He is up to something, he came in and picked a grape and I know he doesn't like grapes,' I thought for a moment, my curious mind came into action and I went back up the hall, looked under the doormat and there it was, a squashed grape. I went back picked another and replaced it. She bunged me another fiver and off I went. Another successful day.

Another day we had a phone call. A big delivery to the CVA in Portland Road, I had to take it to the boardroom. I delivered it and they asked me to take the empties. I went around the back started to load them on and realised there were a few full ones. After I got back I sorted them out and ended up with five bottles of champagne to get rid of. Another good day.

CHAPTER FIVE

I had quite a lot of spare time when delivering because I was told to help out clients as much as possible to keep them sweet. I was very friendly with the café owner, Ted, and I went in there for a fry-up in the mornings. I did about an hour's washing up and did not have to pay, a great agreement. I had a laugh and a joke and it passed an hour. Well this particular morning I went to the shop, picked up my orders, got in the van and went to the café for my breakfast. I was there a good hour or more. I got back in the van looked at my tickets and saw the first one was in Hove — off I go. I pulled up outside, went to the back of the van opened the doors… oh dear! No orders. How do I explain where I have been for the last hour and a half? Well I opened the bonnet, rubbed oil and grease on my hands, went back to the shop and told the manager I had broken down. He then apologised to me for the state of the van. Another good day.

Sometimes I had to go to the brewery and collect items. This was in Waterloo Street, Hove. One morning the manager told me to go and pick up a crate of beer. He said hurry up as the order has to go out as soon as I get back.

Well I put my foot down coming back along the seafront. I was doing about fifty MPH when a couple of kids suddenly ran onto a crossing. I slammed on my brakes and the crate of beer slid from one end of the van to the other. It hit the grid behind my seat and exploded. I was drenched in Brown Ale. I had to go back and get some more, and go home change my clothes and wash. The order was very late!

Another time I went for a crate of beer and some bottles of spirits. I was loading this on when I bent down to pick up a crate of beer. All the floors were very old and made of wood. Well I slid my hand under the crate and felt a sharp pain in my finger, nothing too bad. I had a look and saw a splinter. It had gone under my nail and come out through the front of my finger. The strange thing it didn't hurt so I carried on loading and started to drive back. I got halfway back by Hove Lagoon when wham! The pain hit. I had tears running down my face and so I drove straight up to Hove Hospital. They had a hard job to get it out because the wood was so old it kept breaking. They cut a big V in my nail and dipped my finger into a pot of iodine, bandaged it and I went back to work. I really enjoyed this job but the lure of more money pulled me back to the building site.

I started back with my dad tacking ceilings.

(I think about this time I bought my first motorbike. It was an old Coventry Eagle. It had a square tank. My brother, Frank, decided it needed a service. He took it apart and that was the end of that. I remember the insurance cost 7/6p (about 75p) and the bike would be worth a fortune today).

I soon got fed up with the building site work, the wet and cold. Lunchtime you would put a plank across a couple of breeze blocks and sit on this to eat your lunch. The tea was brewed in a bucket on an open fire, made with real tea leaves, they put the milk in but no sugar. You dipped your tin mug in and got a cup. I have seen paddies cooking eggs and bacon on a shovel and cut the bread with a bow saw. They were animals — lovely blokes but their eating habits were something to be desired!

As I have said I learned plasterboarding when I first started work and I suppose I have handled plasterboards most of my working life.

When I was seventeen I was back working for my father. He would subcontract work to about five of his lads. He had gone to the bank to get the money for the wages and he went into the pub, The Railway Inn in Portslade. He got his pint and went and sat down.

After a few minutes the barman said, "Wake up, Mick, or you will spill your beer," and he was gone. He was fifty-two years old. One of my biggest regrets is I never spoke to him man to man and I never really knew him. They said it was coronary thrombosis. After that brother Frank took over. The problem with Frank was we spent too much time in the cafés on the pinball machines.

One day I went to work with Frank, he had his motorbike and sidecar. I was on the pillion and Vicky Enright was in the chair. We were working in Eastbourne. Well at lunchtime Vicky vanished, we never thought much about it, and at four p.m. we packed up and went home. We got to Lewes and the bike ground to a halt, the clutch had burned out. Well we managed to ring my brother Colin and he came to get us. When we were transferring the tools over Vicky said, "Don't forget this," and out of the boot of the sidecar he dragged this sack full of scrap lead; he had collected it at lunchtime! No wonder the clutch burned out.

One lad we had working with us, his name was Dave, he lived up on the Old Shoreham Road. I often worked with him, he was about six foot tall but he always had these small motors. I remember he had a Messerschmitt, it was a three wheeler and it looked like the body of an aeroplane. The top was a large plastic bubble which swung over the side to allow you to get in and out. We were working down in Midhurst and it had been raining hard all day; when we got to Stopham Bridge it was flooded. I remember us going through the water and the water pouring in. Amazingly the engine kept running; we both ended up with wet arses!

After that he bought an Isetta. It was made in Italy, a very small three wheeled bubble car; you did at least sit next to each other. The front was one large door which swung open to allow you to get in and out. It was very strange having no bonnet in front of you. After that he bought a Fiat Multipla, a conventional car, but still very small.

Another good mate of mine, Alan Smith, we were working down at Butlins in Bognor putting up ceilings. This day we went down in his Berkley three wheeler, it had a small two-stroke engine. On the way down the exhaust blew. Well Alan chatted up the pipe laggers, got some stuff and he lagged the leak on the way home.

We both said at the same time, "Can you still smell that burning?" He pulled over and we both jumped out. We looked under the car and the lagging was smouldering. We ripped it off. I suppose we were very lucky. Another mile and the whole lot would have gone up in flames!

Another time I was driving home from Eastbourne. I had a white Fiat Sports, at the time quite a fast car. I had a bloke working with me, his name was Bert Pulling. He had worked for my dad for years. Just before Lewes there was a short dual carriageway. In the centre of this was a four foot high grass bank. As we approached this there were three cars in a line in front so I decided to overtake them. I pulled out and stuck my foot down. I had almost got alongside of the first car when he decided to pull out and overtake the cars in front. There was nowhere to go but up the bank. It all seemed like in slow motion but we ended up on the roof sliding along the road at about fifty miles an hour. We came to a halt and the other cars had gone!

I said to Bert, "I think we had better get out of this because there's hot oil and water dripping on my legs."

We climbed out of the windows and there were tools and nails all over the road. We gathered up all we could and just then a labourer came running out of this field to see if we were OK. We then pushed it over onto its wheels, the windscreen had gone and the roof was two inches lower. We managed to get the doors open, got back in, turned the key and it started. I then drove it all the way home and all Bert kept on about was the fact that I had broken his flask!!

I took it into the bodyshop and in a week I got it back as good a new.

Cars played a big part of my life. You could not do it now but we would change our cars every couple of months. I hate to think how much money I threw away swapping cars. The shortest time I owned a car was three to four days. I remember it was an Austin Eleven Hundred. The day after I bought it I was coming along the Old Shoreham Road heading west where the Goldstone Football Stadium was. I was only doing thirty-five miles an hour; we had just had a shower of rain, and the car started to slide. I tried to correct it but it went on sliding. It crossed the road, luckily nothing was coming the other way, mounted the pavement and slid into the park trees flashing past. I was waiting for the bang and I came to a halt in between two very large trees. This shook me a bit not being in control, so I took it back and changed it for a Ford Escort. The funny thing was I had to go to Endevers the Ford garage and up the side there was my Austin completely mangled; it had been in a really bad crash. This was only a week later; I think I did the right thing getting rid!

Once I had a lovely Triumph Vitesse, it was a pretty little car, black and white with a soft top, worth quite a bit today but I was coming home from work in London and blew the engine to bits. I got it towed home and then bought another engine from the breaker's yard and fitted it with the help of Derek.

Talking about Derek he was a very sad case of being in the wrong place at the wrong time. He went on holiday on a barge on the Norfolk Broads and while in the middle of nowhere he had a heart attack. No mobile phones then and no one could get to him. He was only about twenty-two years old. If it had happened down here he would have probably survived; he was a really nice guy.

Another one of the lads died very young, Richard, (he was as mad as a box of frogs, he would do anything for a laugh). He would come out for a meal and he would eat the flower display on the table. For a few years we did the boat show at Earls Court and Richard would hire the minibus and it was a great day out. With Richard it only felt like a few weeks between his wedding and his funeral. He taught scuba diving and he was down the West Country with two young lads diving on a wreck. Apparently he signalled to them to come up and when he got to the surface they were not there. He waited for a bit and went down again, meanwhile they surfaced but Richard did not. I think they found his body a few days later, he was quite young also, thirty-two years old I believe.

Last but not least was Jack. He was quite a bit older but was still one of the lads. We went through a time when we had fishing boats and spent many hours fishing which reminds me of the first time Alan Smith, a good friend of mine, and I went boat fishing. We had been beach fishing for years and Alan bought this eight foot dingy. I can't remember if we towed it or kept it on the beach, anyway, we were going fishing. We launched this little dingy, the sea was flat, we had two eight foot beach casters each, two great big fishing boxes. Alan could not swim so he had this fully inflated car inner tube an anchor, a tilly lamp and a small outboard plus a pair of oars. Off we go intrepid fishermen! Not a lot of room but it was loads of fun, we were only a few hundred yards off the beach and it started to get dark so we packed up our gear and decided to come in. The sea had got up a bit and you could hear the waves crashing on the beach.

I said to Alan, "This could be a bit tricky." It was pitch black! "I think the best way to do this is to go full chat at the beach and when we hear it touch jump over the side and drag it up the beach."

What we had forgotten was that to steady the boat we had lowered the dagger board. We heard it touch and both jumped over the side, the water was about seven foot deep. We both disappeared under the water and the next wave swamped the boat. We managed to get the dingy ashore but we had lost almost everything!

CHAPTER SIX

When I was about twenty or twenty-one I was still using the cafes, rock and rolling and riding a motor cycle when I met Ivy. I walked into the café and she was working behind the counter. All the blokes were drooling over her, she was stunning. She was about five foot six, long black hair down to the middle of her back, the perfect figure and a stunning smile. I had a string of on and off girlfriends but nothing serious.

After a couple of weeks one of the lads said, "She fancies you."

I replied, "You're having a laugh!"

About a week later I plucked up the courage to ask her out and to my amazement she said, "Yes."

I think I took her to the White Pigeons in Hove and after a meal we went to the pictures. She shared a flat in Hove with her mate, Anne. Anne had a boyfriend. His name was Bob Dugard. He was quite a good speedway rider, his brothers were also riders. They rode for Eastbourne Eagles. Bob's father owned the speedway track in Arlington, Eastbourne. He also owned a big engineering firm on the Old Shoreham Road in Hove. I think the boys still do manage it. We often drove to race meetings over the South of England; the four of us in the front of the pickup and two speedway bikes in the back. I did have a go myself a couple of times but I valued my life too much. Those boys are mental. I saw many horrific crashes. At Arlington Stadium they also held stock car races. This was also very enjoyable, Demolition Derby and the like. One car that was always winning was a motor car called Yogi Bear. There was quite a lot of winnings to be had.

Ivy worked as a supervisor in an underwear factory, a bit like Coronation Street, and I would pick her up from work. I had a little red sports car then, a Berkley Four Wheeler, a very quick motor. I went out with Ivy for over a year and we decided to get married. Her parents lived on the Isle of Sheppey. By then I had got my compensation for my accident on the boat and so we had a white church wedding. We bought this house in North Road, Portslade, up in the Old Village.

We decided not to have any kids as we were quite happy how we were. I was still working on the building site and things were fine. She had this dog, a pure white Samoyed, it was like a husky. This particular morning, we had both gone to work, and left the back door open so the dog could go out. Well he had got into my shed and found a bag of cement coulour. All you needed was a pinch of it in a gauge of cement. When we got home from work we went into the lounge. The door to the kitchen was glass and everything looked red. I opened the door. I could not believe my eyes, everything was red: the lawn, the borders, the pond, everything in the kitchen, which I had recently decorated! It had been raining and the dog had been swinging this bag of red dye everywhere. In the middle of this mess stood the dog. I could have murdered him! I hosed it all down but I could not get rid of the red. Needless to say there was no way I was taking a bright red dog for a walk!

Ivy and Ann decided to enter Miss Brighton competition. Much to their surprise Ivy won and Ann came second. That started another episode in my life. I would run them all over the South of England doing these beauty competitions. Ivy had many titles and won quite of lot of money tax free. This led to me meeting many good looking girls. I was amazed when they told me that most of them didn't have boyfriends because they said most fellas thought they were out of their league.

At one time there was a film out, it was Walt Disney's His Girl Friday. It just happened that it was at the same time there was an American aircraft carrier in at Southampton. They also run a beauty competition called My Girl Friday, sponsored by Revlon beauty products. Well Ivy won this and the prize was £200 plus some makeup and a night out at Southampton Town Hall. This all sounded very good. I drove her down there and when we went in there was the Mayor and his wife, a few dignitaries and fifteen hundred American sailors and Ivy and me. She was mobbed and had a queue of blokes wanting a dance.

I think that was one of the worst days of my life. About a week later I arrived home from work and there was a lorry unloading this huge crate into my front garden. It was made of wood and was about five foot square. I checked that it was ours and got some tools and started to break it open. It was full of cosmetics, perfume and deodorant. We could have opened a shop and we were giving it away for ages!

It was about this time we decided to go on holiday. We had bought a camping trailer and I had a Sunbeam Rapier. My brother Colin wanted to show us where he was stationed in Germany so we decided to go to the Black Forest. He had a Mini Van at the time. On the ferry going over he got chatting to this German feller; it turned out he used to be a prisoner of war. He was a very nice man and he said he lived in the Black Forest and he said there is a camping place nearby so we agreed to do this. Campsites were very few and far between in those days so we camped anywhere.

One evening it was quite foggy and we found this nice place to pull into. I put my trailer up and Colin pitched his tent. When we woke up in the morning the fog had cleared and to our surprise we were parked in someone's driveway! We made a very quick exit and went on our way.

Another time we were caught in a very big traffic jam; we were there ages and it was dark. We were almost under a flyover so we pulled off the road and because it was easier we just put the tent up. We all got in our sleeping bags, four abreast – me, Ivy, Colin and his wife, Amy. We were all fast asleep when all of a sudden the tent flap opened and there stood two burly policemen with their guns drawn; needless to say we were packed up and out of there like a shot! After we got a unique German rollocking.

We had the address of this German we had met on the boat, it was a place called Nargold, in the Black Forest. We found it on the map and we finally arrived. It was a beautiful little village settled in this valley with a river winding through the middle. The campsite was by the side of this river. When we went in it was so good we were not sure we could afford to stay there. After we had found our spot and settled in we enquired as to where Udolf Graff lived. He pointed to this amazing wooden chalet on the side of the hill and then he told us he worked for him and that Udolf owned the whole valley, all the little houses dotted about were owned by him and were all for his workers. We found out later he also owned a huge saw mill.

Later we went up to his house, it was fantastic; everything was timber at the front it was five storeys high, at the back one storey. He took us in and introduced us to his family, they were all really nice. We all drank beer and spirits. This always sticks in my mind. We also had plain biscuits but they put a square of chocolate on the top. I thought this was very unusual.

He took us all over the place to see the sites and then one day he took us to his saw mill. This was amazing. One machine in particular had a whole tree trunk. It was clamped one end and it was driven into a huge circular saw. This blade was taller than a man, it was amazing to see it slice through a tree like a knife through butter! He made it a fantastic holiday and to top it all when we left the site he wouldn't let us pay. A fantastic holiday.

On the way home we passed quite a lot of American troop convoys. They were amazed at the size of Colin's Mini and would give a toot as we went by. We stopped at this service station for a bite to eat and when we left Colin parked his Mini under one of their lorries and we took some photos.

Ivy's sister lived in Dunstable and I ran her up there a couple of times. I know I had changed my car again and got a Sunbeam Alpine, a two seater, quite quick I remember. We were still doing the beauty circuit. One evening while watching the TV she said, "By the way I have won a holiday in Spain for one and do you mind me going?"

I said, "Of course not."

Anyway off she went, just before she came back this huge bunch of flowers arrived. She said these were all part of the prize, how gullible was I?

Her first night home and she said she had to go out. This started me thinking and still it didn't click. Two days later I was out walking the dog late at night when I saw her sitting in a Mini with this bloke. I walked over to it opened the door a bit rough and ripped one of the hinges off. I dragged him out and I saw red. Ivy was screaming, "Don't hurt him!" I don't know about hurt him I was going to kill him! I let go of him and he got back in his car and somehow managed to close the door. He started it up and shot off, you couldn't see his arse for dust. Ivy came indoors and told me she was leaving me. I was devastated. I was still boiling with anger and I lashed out at the light fitting in the lounge. It smashed into a million pieces and I have another scar to prove it. The next day she packed and left and I never saw her again.

I took a lodger in to help pay the mortgage, Alan was his name, and he fancied himself as a pop group manager. One day he said he had this group and they were based in London and would it be OK if they dossed down for a night. I agreed and when I got home from work that afternoon there was this Rolls Royce Hearse parked outside. I went in and was greeted by five hippies slouched all over the lounge. They stayed for a couple of nights and then they moved on. It turned out they were quite successful. They called themselves The Steam Packet. In the end Alan started up a removal company and did very well.

After Ivy went it hit me quite hard. I didn't want to work, I couldn't sleep, they found me wandering the streets in just my jeans and T-shirt in the pouring rain.

My other mate, Alan, and his wife, Carol, were very good to me; they fed me and pulled me round. They were, and still are, very good friends.

I, meanwhile, got behind with the mortgage. I started going back down the pub and things got back to normal. Work got very scarce and we had a petrol shortage, in fact it went on ration. It got quite scary with no work, I was doing any little job that came along. We heard on the grapevine there was a big job at Southampton. They were building a new hospital and they needed tackers and dry liners. Alan, Ray Fisher and myself pooled our petrol tickets and managed to fill the car up and off we went. When we got there we saw the foreman and he said we could start straight away. Well we loaded all the materials on the job and were just about to start when this fella came in. He was quite chatty and asked us where we had come from. We told him Brighton and then he asked to see our cards. We replied 'what cards?' and he said your Union Cards. We said we weren't in the Union. That was it, his whole attitude changed, within twenty minutes we were escorted off site and told not to come back. This was about the same time as the newspaper strike which got very violent. They were coaching workers from outside London and the Union men were wrecking the buses. The police got involved and it was like a battlefield so we didn't want to upset the Unions. We were really pissed off but there was nothing we could do.

Another time I remember I was working on a house on this farm. It was in the middle of nowhere in Horsham. I was working with Gerald Foss, we only had one room to finish. We were tacking the ceilings and it started to get dark. To put the last three boards up we burned some newspapers so that we could see. We finished it and got in the car and off we went, it was about nine p.m. The narrow concrete road was not illuminated. I was not concentrating and I managed to drop one of the front wheels off the edge. The front of the car just dropped and we ground to a halt. No matter what we did we could not get the car out so I locked it and we started to walk home not realising it was about twenty-three miles. Thank heavens it was a dry night. We ran a bit, then walked a bit, no one would stop.

At about three thirty a.m. we got to the bottom of Snakey Hill and this car pulled up. Two blokes got out, it turned out it was the Chief Inspector and a PC. After we explained what had happened they dropped us home. I thought that was very good of them.

I must mention (Middletons of Lancing), Jimmy Middleton, a contractor who dealt with plasterboarding and he also invented Artex. It was very popular in those days, now of course, most people detest it. It made him a millionaire. He lived in the penthouse above his offices on the Brighton Road, Lancing. He had this black Rolls Royce. I went down there one Friday for my cheque and he was in a terrible mood. He told us that he had put in for a service and apparently they had put it up on the ramp and an apprentice had driven it off the end by mistake. It had completely trashed the front end and he had to use taxis to go everywhere.

One day I got down to the office looking for a job. He said there was a job in Steyning but the boards were still on the lorry. He asked me if I could drive a lorry, I said no but I would give it a go. I climbed up into the cab and Beck got in the other side. It was a Ford Thames Trader. It felt massive and in those days the Norfolk Bridge was much narrower. Off we went and I hoped I wouldn't meet anything coming the other way. Well I did, another lorry, and I had his wing mirror off but I just kept going. We got to Steyning and found the job was in the High Street. I had to back this thing down an alleyway between two shops. I had about six inches either side to spare. Talk about being thrown in at the deep end! I managed to do it. We then unloaded eighty plasterboards. The next day we tacked the ceilings. He only paid us for doing the ceilings but nothing for driving the lorry. He was a tight old git.

While working for Jim Middleton I got to know the Addisons. They were a family of artexers. Just like my old man they were father and four boys about the same age as us. There was even a Colin and Brian and a Graham and of course Keith who later in life became my partner. I must tell you this little story. One of Ivy's mates who did the beauty circuit, she was married to a policeman and had two young boys. I bumped into her when I was shopping and we got chatting. She remarked that I was losing weight and I needed feeding up. She then invited me to dinner after work and one evening I asked her when and she said Thursday, she would cook me a roast dinner.

I finished work early, got home and got cleaned up. I then walked up to their house and she came to the door and invited me in. She said the kids were in bed and her husband was working. I sat down and started watching the telly; five minutes later the kitchen door opened and there she stood, a tray in her hand and nothing on except her high heels! She had a fantastic body and needless to say I never got to eating dinner. I had a fantastic evening and I went home knackered. About four days later there was a knock on the door, when I opened it there she stood with two suitcases and two small boys. She blurted out that she had left her husband and wanted somewhere to stay. I invited her in and of course we ended up in bed. She was Scottish and had flaming red hair. What I didn't know was how quick she tried to organise my life. She told me how much housekeeping money she needed and most of all how she wanted ginger twins. I think she stayed two or three days and I told her it was not working and I think she went back to her husband. I don't know what happened to her but I never saw her again.

It was all too much too quick, I was still thinking a lot about Ivy and I was having problems working so I was getting deeper in debt with the mortgage and the rates. I remember Alan and I thought everybody was in the same boat and when we both got a summons for non-payment of rates we thought there would be dozens of people there. When we turned up at the Court we were the only two there and when we went in one of the magistrates said because you have no money it's no excuse not to pay your rates. We were both fined and told to pay weekly.

Not long after that four of us were working on this chalet bungalow in Bognor and on the way to work one of the lads was all excited about his dagger he had just acquired. His name was Vicky Enright and he collected all military stuff. I was standing at the top of the stairs, at the time I was holding my hand flat in front of me with this commando's knife laying on it with the point pointing at my stomach. Well all of a sudden one of the other lads came around the corner with a plasterboard. As he swung it around the end of the board hit the handle of the dagger, it felt like someone had punched me (no real pain).

Anyway I had my hand around it and Vicky said, "Don't muck about."

I said, "I'm not."

I pulled it out and the claret spurted out. Poor old Vic went a funny colour, someone ran out and told the foreman who then rang the ambulance. They took me to Chichester Hospital and I had one hell of a job to convince them that it was an accident. I was in there for a couple of months, another close shave!

Another time Colin and I were working down at Polegate on a site of new houses. We were tacking the ceilings. I remember it was raining hard and all around this house was thick mud and outside of this house was a small cupboard. Colin said he'd push the board over if I went outside and fixed it. I agreed and out I went. I was about to climb on a trestle when Colin pushed the board over, the top course of bricks were loose and came crashing down straight on my head. I must have been dazed because Colin was shouting at me why wasn't I fixing the board? I was outside staggering around in the mud with a four inch cut in my head. What with all the rain I was covered in blood and mud. Someone said there was a doctor around the corner as Eastbourne Hospital was miles away. We walked around to the doctor's, opened the door and all the patients took one look and said in one voice "YOU GO FIRST!" I think I had six stitches in that one. The funny thing was three days later I was back in there. I had slipped with my knife and gashed my hand. The doctor said to numb it he would have to stick the needle in so he might as well sew it up without it so I sat there and watched him put four stitches in my hand.

When the tacking got short it seemed that the dry liners had plenty of work so I watched a couple for half a day and thought 'it's not a lot different to tacking'. The only difference being they stuck it and we nailed it. I managed to get one of the contractors to let me dry line this house. Well I locked myself in this house. It took me three days to do it and when the gaffer came down to check it he found nothing wrong so from then on I was tacker and dryliner. I did this for quite a few years.

CHAPTER SEVEN

It was about this time I was introduced to Mags (Margaret, my second wife). Gerald, my mate, she was his girlfriend's friend. After our first date I didn't think I would see her again. I remember we went to the pictures, the Granada in Hove. Someone had driven us there, when we pulled up outside, I got out and like the gentleman that I am I was going to go around and open her door. Well I slammed the door shut but unbeknown to me she had slid across and caught the full force of me slamming my door in the face. I think I spent all evening apologising to her.

After that things got better, they must have done because when she got pregnant for the second time we decided to get married. My first was a boy and we named him Paul. I had got behind with the mortgage and lost the house and we were living with Mag's mother in one room, the two of us and the baby. It was not for long as we got a flat in Downland Court. Luckily the block we were in was good. We had heard rumours about the place. We were in a top floor flat, four storeys high, a bit difficult for Mags with the pushchair.

I must confess I was not the perfect husband in those days. There was the darts team at the pub two nights a week and Sunday lunchtimes in the pub. The rest of the time I was working where I could find it. Oh I forgot the fishing. Almost every weekend I was down the boat. I never actually owned one but I was always working on someone's when we were not fishing. There were plenty of fish out there to catch in those days. That was before all the Belgium and Spanish trawlers dragged everything up. Everyone complained about how close to the shore they came but nothing was done about it. They completely killed off the fishing.

Prior to that there was a group of us that fished. There was Alan and myself, Bob and Richard and Chris and Slippery. There was Ray, Jack, Keith and Dereck. Yes we all fished, drank and partied together. The parties were good, any excuse to have a party we all had them at different mates' homes. We would drink, dance and natter. At about midnight the slow music would come on and the lights would go out and you would end up with someone else's wife snogging. No one ever ran off with anyone else's partner, it was just good fun.

My brother, Colin, had got married and moved to Polegate and he had heard of this country club up the road from him at the Upper Dicker so we thought we would try it. It was magic, they had a five piece group, a dance floor, chicken in a basket and best of all a swimming pool. It was called Deanland Wood. We would form a convoy every Saturday evening usually four or five cars. We would dance some more then end up in the swimming pool. We would leave at about midnight and drive home (no drink and drive then). Sometimes we would race (bad news). One evening on the way home we turned around this bend and there was Dereck in this field, he hadn't made the bend, had gone through the fence, he had a Ford Anglia and he had put a much bigger engine in it but he hadn't uprated the brakes. We all got out and pushed him out. We were all laughing and fooling about, we were all covered in mud. Poor old Dereck he took some stick after that.

Driving through Lewes once we were actually stopped by a policeman. We were all over the top with drink. All he wanted to know was where we had been and where we were going.

It was about this time we were offered a council house in Easthill Drive. I knew the area very well, the properties were all individual and it didn't look like a council estate, three bedrooms, a large back garden and a front garden. They said we could move in after three weeks as they had to redecorate it. I told them to forget the decorating and I would do it, and we moved in straight away. It even had a garage. I had been doing lots of work for friends knocking two rooms into one, plastering, hanging doors and general carpentry I was learning as I went along.

I got to know this fella who had a second-hand shop in Trafalgar Road in Portslade, Harry Davis, a typical Jewish wheeler dealer. He always gave me a good deal. He asked me to hang a couple of doors. I agreed and down I went. I hung his doors and it just progressed from there. It was, 'can you do this and can you do that'.

He had this huge house in Portland Road. I knocked a few walls down and did quite a lot of plastering but the piece de resistance was the chimney he wanted taking down. It was huge. It fed four fireplaces. They were back to back, two up in the bedrooms and two separating the two lounges. They were monsters. I got Keith to give me a hand. We both got up on the roof and we started taking it down, the bricks we dropped down inside but the chimney pots had to be carried down. That was a bit hairy with no scaffold. I think we filled six skips with bricks. When we finished it was like looking up a lift shaft. Keith knew what he was doing so he attacked the roof and I concentrated on the ceilings and floors. When I had started the lounge ceilings Harry came in and said he'd changed his mind, I thought, 'on no'. He said he didn't want it all rebuilt, just the lounge and the back room knocked into one. Another RSJ required, this was about fourteen feet when we were fitting it. I remember I was in shorts. Keith and I were inching our way up the steps, me one end and him the other. I was on a pair of wooden steps and had almost got to the top when the step snapped with the weight. As I came down the steps snapped one by one, the problem was a couple of the nails that held the steps went straight down my legs; another trip to the Hove Hospital.

I suppose we were lucky never badly hurt. I was always a bit of a chancer, when I was getting to the end of the job Harry and his wife moved in to one room and I had to wait for them to go out so that I could finish off. When I was working in there I noticed there was a photo of Harry's wife, well I took a label from one of the rolls of fibreglass and stuck it on the photo. It said, 'For safety's sake keep this bag away from children!' He laughed like a drain but she was not amused. She didn't talk to me for a week after that.

One day I went in and Harry said he had disconnected a power box in the kitchen above the door, could I concrete it?

"Yes," I said, "no problem."

I turned off the power under the stairs and then went and got my crowbar and hacksaw. I then got up the steps, prised it off the wall, got my hacksaw and cut it. There was a flash and a bang, it blew the hacksaw to bits and threw me across the room. I had a small burn on my hand but no real harm.

When I finished Harry's, his next-door neighbour came and asked me if I would do some work for him. This probably was the best time I had ever, his name was Joe Mackari and he asked me in, stuck a double scotch in my hand and introduced me to the rest of the family. There was his wife, Jean, who was lovely, his two daughters, Gloria and Maria, and his son, Anthony. The same thing really it started with little jobs and it just escalated. I worked in his factory, his shop in the West End, his house in New Church Road, Hove, and in his new house on The Kings Way, Hove. Joe was a very wealthy man and didn't suffer fools. He was also a very talented musician. He could get a tune out of any instrument but his main one was the saxophone.

The two girls played guitar and piano and the boy played drums and they all sung. All the aunts and uncles had been on the stage or were impersonators. Christmas parties were amazing, everybody did a turn. Gloria, or Glo as she liked to be called, and her boyfriend as he was the would do gigs out and about playing guitar and singing. They also wrote songs for the group called The Love Affair and they had a couple of Top Ten hits.

Back to the work. Joe asked me if I could build an extension for him so I did some drawings and off I went. I marked out footings and started digging. Joe had a look and said it would be great. I carried on digging, I had to go down to four foot. On the second day I had almost got it all out when Jean came out and brought me a cup of tea. I climbed out of the trench and was drinking my tea when there was a rumble and the part I was working in collapsed. It had broken my fork and pick in half.

If I had been in there it would have been my legs. Another close call!

When I first started jobbing building I made general mistakes but nothing I couldn't put right. I know one crazy thing I did but luckily got away with it was I had to take the lounge wall out so that the extension was part of the lounge so I jacked up the ceiling with a couple of arrows for support and then started to take the wall down so that I could fit the RSJ where I thought I had measured it correctly but I was mistaken. I kept measuring it and chopping a bit more out. Jean asked me if I would like a cup of tea, well I got down off the scaffold and looked up to see there was nothing holding the back of the house up. We got that RSJ in double quick!

I had finished building it and was painting the outside when this fella looked over the fence and asked if the owner was in. I told him yes and said go around to the front where Joe answered the door. He said he was the Building Inspector. Joe asked him in and worked his magic on him with the help of a bottle of scotch. We never saw him again.

I built an extension on his garage so that he could get his motor in it and the following evening I got a phone call, could I pop down and have a look. All kind of things went through my mind but when I got down there Jean had backed her car straight through it. She forgot it had been extended two feet; another job to sort out.

As I was saying Joe was a bit eccentric. He had been to an auction and he said, "I've got some bits coming this afternoon, can you put them in the garage?" This lorry turned up and we unloaded fifty motorised mowers, only three of them worked. He had paid thirty quid for the lot. So I spent the next two days fixing lawn mowers. I think we ended up throwing about ten away but he sold the rest for thirty-forty pounds a time, not bad eh? He could sell anything.

I saw him working his best one day. I was working with Chris and we were building a window display in his shop in Charing Cross Road in the West End. It was a huge shop and was full of new and second-hand musical instruments. He had about five staff and the shop was busy all the time and was often frequented by pop stars of the time. Joe knew everyone. This particular day this limousine pulled up outside and this man came in. Joe grabbed him and he said he wanted to buy a clarinet for his daughter. He said he only wanted a cheap one as his daughter was only learning.

Joe asked if she was in the car. He nodded so Joe replied, "Fetch her in," which he did. He said to her, "Play what you have learned." She played and it was awful, but Joe said to this bloke, she is good and got lots of potential, she would really benefit if she had a good clarinet and he sold the bloke a £450 one. It was magic to watch.

Joe's factory was in North London and again was a large building. He wanted me to build some workbenches. When I arrived Joe met us and we were greeted by an articulated lorry full of second-hand doors. There were well over a hundred by the time we had unloaded. It was time to go home. He also said the roof was leaking a little but having been a roofer that was no problem. Dereck and I decided to stay up there until the job was finished so we packed our sleeping bags and off we went. The idea was to cut one door in half, nail another to the top of the two halves. There were his blokes in there too. Well we had done a length about fifty yards long; we were going great guns or so we thought. As we finished someone leaned on the end one and the first one collapsed and the weight of the first one set off a chain reaction and down they went like a pack of cards. The next day was spent making corner spaces and fixing them. We got the piss taken out of us for that little episode.

In the factory they made pedals for electric guitars (Wow Wow and Fuzz and many more). They also made small practice amps for electric guitars, the trade name was Coulorsound. I played a little bit of guitar and thought I would like an amp. That evening Dereck being a whizz with electronics assembled one which I took home with me. I told Joe about six months later, and he admired my ingenuity, said "Well done," and laughed.

Joe treated me like a son. Every Friday I would work late so that I would be there when he got back from London. I would give him my bill and he would put his hand in his back pocket and pull out a bundle of notes. He would always overpay me. He would tell Jean to get me a Scotch and then promptly tear up my receipt. One evening I overstayed talking about work and music and it was getting late and I had quite a few drinks and when I went out to the van it would not start, flat battery!

Joe said, "Take mine." It was a classic red Mercedes convertible with leopard skin upholstery.

I said," Joe, I've been drinking."

He said, "No matter, take it, it's Sunday tomorrow and I don't need it."

I got in it and drove it home. The next day I took it down the pub and showed the lads. I told them it was mine. Anyway after lunch I took Mags and the kids to Polegate (Colin's place) with the top down. I felt like a millionaire. After that experience I bought several convertibles, in fact I drive one now!

Going over to Polegate was a bit of a ritual after the pub on Sunday lunchtime. I would have lunch, get Mags and the kids and off we would go. One Sunday could have ended up a disaster. What happened was I got home from the pub and was finishing my dinner when I yelled up to the kids to get ready. Usually they would finish what they were doing and rush downstairs and pile into the car. This particular day Karen took a bit longer, the next thing I heard her screech. I rushed upstairs and the room was full of smoke; there was a large cardboard box full of books and it was alight. I opened the bedroom window, grabbed the box and threw it out into the back garden. What had happened was an antiquated electric fire, which was flush fitted and had never worked all the time we had been there. This box of books had been pushed up against it, Kazzy had finished her book and thrown it on the pile of books in the box. It had slid down the back and pushed the switch down and turned the fire on, she had stayed to pick another book, well you know the rest… If she had run down the stairs and got in the car I think we might have come home to a surprise.

It was a lovely house, a bit dated and I spent a lot of time working and modernising it. The first thing I did was to build a stone fireplace. It was the length of the room, very low with a copper canopy.

Each side there were two low shelves which the stereo sat on, under them were two matching display openings which were illuminated. It looked really good but today it would be the first thing you would rip out.

The next thing I did was to knock a hole between the lounge and the dining room. I measured it and built a cabinet the other side and in the opening I fitted the fish tank so you could see it from both sides. One day Karen and

I were at home and Mags had gone to work so we got in the car and went down B&Q. We got some emulsion paint and wallpaper. When we got back I painted the ceiling while Kaz was stripping the wallpaper, then we did the gloss and with her help we did the paperhanging. We cleared everything up and hoovered and when Mags got home we were sitting in the front room and she could not believe her eyes.

I did many things on impulse. I walked past a shop one day and saw this black and while goatskin rug. I thought it looked brilliant so I went in and bought it. It wasn't until a few days later we had this strange smell in the lounge, I realised in the end it was this rug so it went straight in the bin!

I had accumulated loads of building stuff while I was jobbing and I had loads of ideas. One day I thought I could do the kitchen, I had an almost new hob and oven and loads of other bits I had taken out of other jobs. When Mags came home from work the wall between the back room and the kitchen had gone. The oven was in the middle of the room, there was brick dust and rubble everywhere. I bricked up the back door and in a couple of weeks it was all finished. Everybody who saw it said it was stunning. I built it all. New cabinets with mahogany doors, the door and splash backs were done in dark red, a new hob and eye level oven, all new worktops with a breakfast bar. The best bit of all was the ceiling. I fitted a double suspended ceiling, the central four panels were illuminated, all my mates called it the Wimpy Bar! I also took out the back window and fitted patio doors which I had got off a job in Horsham. We had a cupboard at the top of the stairs so I turned it into a shower, all the time I was busy I was happy, the more difficult the job the more I liked it.

I thought I would put in some slabs and make a hard standing in the front of the house. I dug it out and then I had a word with my mate, Chris, who worked down the docks who could get me some ballast. The next day I awoke to a very loud noisy racket. I looked out of the front window to see this huge lorry drive off; he had tipped a load of ballast in the front. When I went downstairs you could not look out the front window, the pile was so high. I was giving it away for weeks. When I saw Chris he said he had put one bucket on and he thought it was not enough so he put another on. He was obviously taking the piss. He still winds me up about it today.

It takes a lot for me to lose my temper but talking about my driveway reminds me of when one evening my Karen was saying goodnight to her boyfriend and I looked out of the window and they were standing by the brick pier at the end of the front drive. I had just sat down when there was a hell of a crash. I got up and looked out again and there was a car wrapped around the brick pillar. I could not see the kids, my heart dropped. I rushed out and they were in the porch both were really shook up. All the neighbours had rushed out and the driver got out laughing and joking. I am afraid I lost it. I was going to kill him but three of my neighbours had to drag me off of him, he had just come out of the pub at the top of the road and he had lost it on the bend. He was pissed as a rat. Shortly the law arrived and carted him off.

One day Joe told me he had bought a house on the seafront, would I come with him to see it. It was on the corner of Wish Road and the Kingsway. The first thing that struck me was the size, the other thing was the big sign in the front — it read The Seamans Mission. It was huge. I worked on that house for over a year. I did that house from top to bottom. I artexed all the ceilings (it was the rage then)! I put in a new kitchen, decorated, knocked down walls and built new ones, made his garage larger and the biggest job by far was the slabbing at the front and back gardens. I had dug it out and ordered the scalping which went under the slabs for the back, they said that it would be delivered Thursday or Friday. I had gone home on Friday when I got a phone call from Joe, he said get down here quick. I went down and the lorry had tipped the lot in the road, it had blocked Wish Road. I went in Joe's and made some phone calls. In a quarter of an hour four of my mates had turned up armed with shovels and wheelbarrows. When we finished it was dark, about quarter to ten. Joe came out with the beers and everyone was happy.

It was about this time that Glo and Roger decided to get married. Mags and I were invited. We went to the church and then to the reception which was held at the Hotel Metropole, very posh. When we went in they were announcing the people as they arrived. The man on the door announced us, "Mr and Mrs Winstanley, the family builders." One of Joe's little jokes. The best joke he ever pulled off was at the reception, the dance floor had been cleared except for a very small table with a dish on it. Glo and Roger were in the middle ready for the first dance when Roger's brother walked on. Joe had given him a mobile mike and when he gave a speech at the end he said, "Now that Glo is married he would not need Glo's front door keys," and he dropped it in the dish. When one of the guests said he would not need his, then up got another and said he would not need his. This went on for ages; the place was in uproar. Joe had given a key to almost every bloke in the room!

Joe had bought them a flat just along the road and I did a lot of work in it. One day I got this bag of cement out of the van. I had it on my shoulder, I had the front door keys in my hand and I had to do a sharp right and go up the stairs. I tripped and the bag of cement went down. I did not realise at the time but it had pushed the yale key right through my thumb, that was another trip to the hospital!

While we were living in Easthill Drive I went through many cars. I had two Cortinas. I think I started with a Frog Eye Sprite. When I bought it, it was a wreck but I knew Jeff Elms, he owned a small garage down by Portslade seafront. Well between us we did it up, we had to extend the wheel arches to take the eight inch wheels at the back and the sevens on the front. We put in a bigger engine with a shorrock supercharger. I had it reupholstered and sprayed yellow. It was quite a head turner, it went like shit off a stick but we didn't upgrade the brakes so it was a pig to stop!

One day I pulled in the garage and my eyes lit up, there in the back was an orange GP Beach Buggy, being the poser I am I had to have it. And so I found the owner, had a chat and before I knew it, I had done a straight swap. What a prat I was. It was the first one in Sussex, small front wheels and huge ones on the back with a VW engine.

I was down Gerald's one evening discussing work and it started to rain. Well it didn't just rain it larruped down. We could hear it on the window and I looked out and saw the engine looked like someone was playing a hose on it, it was completely exposed at the back. I thought I would have to walk home. Anyway I got in it, turned the key and away it went. I thought brilliant! But I didn't expect what happened next, I got to the end of the road, put my brakes on and this tidal wave came from the back to the front and swamped my feet. I was lucky nothing was coming because I could not or did not stop and carried on across the main road. As soon as I could I drilled some holes in the rear footwells. The soft top leaked like a sieve. In actual fact it was a bit of a dog.

At this time Mags was pregnant with Graham and as she got bigger she found it harder to get in it because there were no doors. One had to slide over the side, not very practical so I decided to get rid of it but nobody wanted it so I put an advert in the paper to swap it for a saloon car. I only had one reply and this fella said you might not want it, it's a Jag. When I went to see it I was amazed, it was a Mark Ten, it was huge. It was one of the largest motors on the road at that time. It was silver with leather seats and a walnut dash.

I decided to do the swap, after the buggy it was enormous. It had a bench seat at the front and when Mags got in, unlike the buggy where you were rubbing shoulders, I could put my arm out and not reach her. It was quite old but very luxurious. I loved driving it the bonnet looked nine miles long after the two foot one on the buggy. It was a bit thirsty but when you saw the size of the engine you could understand why.

I went in the garage one day, they had attendants who filled your car in those days. He filled up the tank and I drove off. I got halfway home when it ground to a halt. I found a phone box and rang Jeff, he came out straight away, checked the carbs and this was diesel not petrol. It was lucky because the car had twin tanks so he flushed it through, switched to the other tank and away it went. I drove back to the garage and they were full of apologies and they took the car, drained it off and then they filled both tanks with petrol to compensate. I had this Jaguar for a long time and I was subcontracting for ABC Dry Construction. I ended up taking six blokes up to London every day. This was before the motorway was built and early in the morning there was hardly any other traffic and I would throw that motor around the many roundabouts, it was good fun.

We were still a bit crazy in those days. One day we caught up the two bosses, Colin and Barry, they were in the pick up truck and they had stopped at the roundabout. I got up behind them and nudged them out onto the busy roundabout; they were panicking but we all thought it very funny.

Another time we were taking it easy when Colin and Barry pulled alongside us and emptied a bottle of water over my windscreen. Later we caught them up and Bec emptied a cup of tea over theirs. Even with their wipers on they couldn't see a thing and they had to stop. In those days you did anything for a laugh.

One thing we did (someone would leave their tobacco tin on the windowsill) was to empty out their tobacco and screw the tin to the windowsill then put the baccy back in it. Beck always brought a radio in. We were tacking timber studwork (all the walls), someone thought it was amusing to leave his radio in-between the two plasterboards, and when it was time to go home Beck could hear it but he could not find it. Eventually we had to give in and took one of the boards off revealing the radio. Poor Beck he was usually the brunt of all the jokes. Someone found a field mouse and put it in his empty lunchbox. Apparently his wife went mad when she opened it and the mouse jumped out! Another time I found a dead sparrow. Beck's coat was hanging on a nail and I put the sparrow in his top pocket with the head sticking out. We were working local at the time so Beck went home on the bus. It wasn't noticed until he got home, he said he had some funny looks from people but nobody told him.

CHAPTER EIGHT

On Easter Sunday the local pubs would get a team together and they would hold a race on the canal. There was a team of eight, two people in the boat at a time. There were five teams and they would row up to the turning bay and back but before the next two could go they had to down a pint of beer, not easy when you are puffing and panting. The winning team got a small barrel of beer. We rowed for the King's Head, Southwick, but we never won.

We were all into fishing in a big way but that's another story... One Saturday we were messing about with the boats when this group of fellas turned up with this strange looking craft. We had a closer look and realised it was a bath with floats. a couple of seats and two pairs of oars. We started talking to them and they explained they were doing the Adur Bathtub Race the following week. We found out the name of the organiser and he told us the rules and said we could enter a team if we had time.

In one week we got a cast iron bath, we used empty oil cans for floats and it was painted GPO Yellow. The race went from Bramber down to Coronation Green, Shoreham. There were only six or seven tubs in the race. We had raised some sponsor money for the RNLI, we put the tub in the water and the race started. Two lads in the tub and the rest were running down the bank. The trouble was when the two rowers were knackered so were the two lads who were to take over. The floats leaked and it started to take in water and we had to drag it out and empty out the water. The paint hadn't had time to dry and we were covered in yellow paint. At the end of the day we were all knackered and covered in mud. We had had a great time and we would all do it again the following year. As the time approached we were ready, we had built a new tub, we had a shallow cast iron bath and the flotation was polystyrene and then fibreglass. We got Watneys Red Barrel to sponsor us and painted the tub blue with Watneys writing on the side. We all got clowns' outfits and we bought two hundred coloured balloons. We got a gas bottle with helium and spent all day filling the balloons. We kept them in my garage overnight. Sunday morning we had the parade through the town, there were about fifteen teams, the word had obviously got around. There was a band leading the parade and we all had collection boxes. If people put something in we would give them a balloon. We would go in the shops and offices, we even went in the funeral parlour. It was great fun.

We went into one café and right at the back was this little old lady, she called me back and put something in the tin and then asked for a kiss. I obliged and was about to leave when she said, "Where's my balloon?" with the biggest toothless grin you have ever seen!

The Moppets.

Our tub was a bit special, we had a pair of blow up women's legs mounted on the front and it even had a car stereo complete with twelve volt battery and twin speakers! I think we came second that year but because of the way we were dressed we got all the press, even a television interview on Southern. There was one disappointment though, Watneys let us down. Although we gave them loads of advertising, all they gave us was a small barrel of beer, so much for their sponsorship!

The following year we were discussing what theme to do and someone suggested The Muppets. We realised the costumes would be impossible and Dereck suggested doing a play on words and calling ourselves The Moppits. We agreed it was a good idea, the costumes were no problem, all dressed up as old washer women and Dereck supplied the mops, care of the BPO. We had the dresses, the tabards, headscarves, tights, curlers and blow up boobs, even the makeup – we looked fantastic and the crowd and the press loved us, we were in the local papers every year. We started winning races and that was more reason to get in the local rags.

One year we had a group of cheerleaders and the one in the front had this lance which she twirled and threw in the air and caught, so I decided to march with her and copy her moves with my mop. The crowd loved it, that was the best parade we ever had. The numbers of entrants increased every year and the last race we did there were over a hundred tubs and the crowds lining the riverbanks was amazing. One year we had just won the race when we were asked if we could show the firemen from Littlehampton how to organise a race from Arundel to Littlehampton. We did this and the first race we entered we won.

Well, we were sitting in the pub discussing the races when somebody said what can we do next and someone said what about doing the Channel. We all agreed to do it and so Dereck and I made enquiries and got a support organised and the lifeboat agreed to come halfway and we agreed a date. The only modification we had to make was to build a higher prow. We had no worries about the tub. We had filled it with water and it didn't sink. The local newspapers got hold of it and we even got an interview with the television. We turned up at the Lighthouse Beach with the tub and the television crew turned up. The presenter was Kate Adie.

We were only there twenty minutes when this traffic warden turned up, a proper jobsworth! "You can't park there," he yelled and we told him it was all to raise money for the Lifeboat. It made no difference so the interview was shorter than we had hoped. We had still got on the box though!

We arrived down at Dover and met the support crew. They informed us that the sea was too rough and we could not attempt it, thank heavens. The next morning the sea was as flat as a pancake, we got towed out of the harbour and around the corner to the beach. Bob and I started to row. I remember looking up at the cliffs. We rowed for an hour and looked up and the cliffs were still there!

I thought, "Oh dear, we have done the wrong thing here!" but just then the tide turned and we were on our way. There were eight of us and we took it in turns to row each hour. We saw the ferries and they saw us and waved and cheered us on. I must admit some of those supertankers were huge and when they went by they pushed out a huge bow wave which reached us ten minutes later. It was quite exciting, we had never used the tub in waves before.

Eleven hours later we reached shore, not Calais as we thought but Cape Grenade, we were all knackered and we put the tub in the support boat and motored back to Dover. Although the telly and newspapers reported it the Guinness Book of Records thought it was foolhardy and said they would not put it in their book because they did not want to encourage anyone else to do it! It has been done since but never with a cast iron bath. At least we raised some money for the lifeboat. Finally we donated the tub to the Girl Guides. I forgot to mention the names of the lads, we were all fishing or working friends, there was Dereck Elicker, Alan Smith, Chris Bunby, Bob Cheesman, Steve Rider, the Guile Brothers, Greg and Martin and myself, eight in all. We all agreed it was one of the hardest things we had ever done, it took us hours of hard graft.

Back to the boats and the fishing… In those days there was loads of fish in the sea, one of my biggest regrets in my life was the fact that I killed so many fish needlessly. We would go out miles to catch tope — they were like small sharks, you could catch them up to thirty pounds. They were great sport. The thing was you could not eat them and invariably we would kill them. I don't really know why I can remember seeing the whole of the floor of the boat covered with skate, beautiful, big black bream and the mackerel were suicidal. You could put a string of feathers on you and pull mackerel up six at a time. I would catch so many I gave them away to the people up the street. When you came home the next evening all you could smell was frying fish.

After the Channel.

Bob, Alan, Steve, Greg, Chris, Brian, Derek, Martin.

Alan and I tried long lining once, we spent hours making it. We made the floats and the weights and got this length of line and fixed one hundred hooks on it. The weekend came and we got it ready. We baited all the hooks, loaded it on the boat and off we went. We went out of the harbour and turned right. Everything was going well until we dropped it over the side, it sank like a stone and we never saw it again (we were full of good ideas).

Another time we were doing some trammelling, this had weights and floats (dan poles with flags) either end and we had learned from the long lining they were long enough. We had bought some nets, they were like curtains which hung under the sea. We would throw the weights and buoys over the side of the boat and then feed the nets over the side. This worked well and we caught loads of fish.

Then we had another bright idea; because the nets filled up half of the boat we decided to tow a dinghy behind us and put the nets in it. Well we got to the harbour mouth and a wave hit it and it capsized shooting the nets all over the harbour mouth. There were boats, yachts and all sorts trying to get by. The fishermen on the quay were yelling at us and we had the coastguard on the tannoy; it was quite embarrassing. We managed to drag it all in the boat and I think that was the last time we used nets for fishing.

One summer's evening Alan and I were coming in after a good day fishing, the sun was just about to dip over the horizon, I was sitting on the stern steering when this pod of dolphins came right alongside us and we could touch them and we even fed them some mackerel. It was a magic moment.

I remember one day the fog came down so thick you could barely see four or five yards in front. We had lost our bearings and we came in very slowly by Worthing Pier. Alan had this boat it was named 'Swift', a converted lifeboat. Anyway I built a cuddy on it and we would use it quite a lot. Well Alan sold it and I think that's when I bought my speedboat. Alan had the Argus delivered and on the front page the headline read 'Jack Hargreaves rescued from sinking boat' He was a presenter on TV and he did fishing programs. The picture was of this submerged boat with just the cuddy above the water. I had to look twice as I recognised the cuddy as the one I had built, poor old 'Swift' had gone down. The problem with these fishing boats was that they were so slow we had to motor for two hours, fish for two hours and then motor back for two hours so that we would not miss the locks.

Keith decided to buy a Dory, a very stable fibreglass boat and with a sixty horsepower outboard it was very fast. It was sixteen foot long and he had it on a trailer, we could launch it down at Ropetackle Public Hard. There were only a few hours either side of low tide that we could not launch, this was great. In ten minutes we could get to the harbour mouth and in an hour we were miles out. This gave us loads of fishing time; it was also exciting bouncing from one wave to the next.

One evening Keith and I decided we would do some night fishing to catch some cod. Obviously it was in the winter and I have never been so cold in all my life; we ended up cuddling up together to keep warm! The boat had no cuddy so it was like sitting in a large plastic bath. We were freezing and to top it off we didn't catch a thing! One good thing came out of using the Dory though… one day coming back from fishing someone said you could probably water-ski behind this. That started the old grey matter working that weekend. I bought a second hand pair of skis, a rope and a bridle. I asked several people about skiing and the next weekend after a bit of fishing we came in to Shoreham Beach and we had a go. How much sea water was swallowed that afternoon I hate to think! It finally clicked that you had to give it full throttle to lift you out. That afternoon I think that we all managed to get up on the skis for a while after that. The fishing took a back seat. After watching a couple of videos of water skiing I had to learn to do monoing (skiing on one ski). It was quite difficult at first and costly as I found out. At first I would transfer my weight onto one leg and signal to Keith and then kick one ski off. Keith would then take the boat in a big circle and then pick the ski up; sometimes it would be a bit choppy and we lost a couple and they were not cheap to replace. I devised a way to get over this problem. I would be up on two skis and then I would bend down grab the back of the binding and swing it up over my shoulder. This worked quite well until I learned to get up on one ski, Keith's Dory would pull up two skiers at a time, that was good fun learning to cross over.

Bob went and bought this big jet boat, it had a Ford engine. Bob being Bob took it out and put a Jaguar three point eight litre engine in it. There was no room for the silencer so when it started up you could hear it in Worthing! It sent a flame out the exhaust a foot long, it had to have a wire bridle on the back because the ordinary one kept melting. It would pull up six skiers at a time easily. We had some fun with that. I still have a vision of Alan on the skis. He could not swim but he could keep himself afloat with a kind of doggy paddle. I thought he was very brave because we would just throw him over the side with a pair of skis on. He left his socks on and his trousers and a blue and white striped T-shirt. Most of the lads by this time had bought wet suits.

I did buy this little eight foot polystyrene dory, it had fibreglass saddle over the back end to make it strong enough to take an outboard motor. I bought a forty horse power mercury engine. That was so much fun. When it was a bit choppy it would actually take off. I was thinking about getting a bigger engine and I rang the makers to see what they recommended. They said I must be barmy as it was designed to take a four horse power engine. Eventually it just broke in half. I managed to salvage the engine but the rest was trashed and so it went to the tip.

After that I bought a Shakespeare speed boat and the merk I fitted on it was orange and white and I called it 'OK Nob'. This was because when I was in the sea ready to get up on the skis that's what they would yell. I got this nickname I suppose because of my ginger hair, Ginger Nob.

I would make people smile when they asked how I got my nickname, I would tell them that my mother only had one arm and she had to get me out of the bath somehow (joke).

One year Alan and I hired a couple of caravans down at Rockley Sands near Poole Harbour. There was Alan, his wife Carol, their two young girls Mandy and Sue, and myself, Mags, our son Paul and our daughter Karen. I was towing the boat behind my Ford Cortina. When we arrived Mags started to unpack when she realised she hadn't packed any of my clothes or shoes. All I had was what I stood up in. Luckily, we had super weather so it was shorts and T-shirts so we bought a couple of pairs of each and that was all I needed.

My First Speedboat

The caravans overlooked the bay, there was a small club which put on entertainment in the evenings. There was a small sandy beach, it was like heaven. There was a slipway for the boat and a beach for the kids.

One day Carol said she would like to learn to water ski. It was ideal because the water was only chest high. Alan stayed in the water with her and showed her what to do, I was driving the boat. I crept out slowly and we got the line tight, it was perfect. I yelled to her, "Whatever you do don't let go." I should not have said this because she didn't. She fell forward and I can still see it now... this wall of water and this face peering through it, eyes like saucers. I had to stop before she drowned. Alan and I laughed so much we were crying. I don't know why but she wouldn't have another go!

Something else we found out was to slow down before you hit the beach. We found this little island all secluded. We ferried the girls over and then the kids. We had packed lunch. After having a ski session I was driving the boat and I didn't slow down approaching the beach. I thought it would slow when it hit the sand but it didn't, we carried on across the sand up the beach and into the bushes and trees. We were lucky we didn't hit a tree full on otherwise we might still be there now! Actually it was a great holiday and I believe that was where my Graham was conceived. We didn't have proper holidays, we had days out together mainly because I was self-employed and if I didn't work I didn't get paid.

I still had this thing in my head about getting a proper job. I was offered a job at Doric Asbestos, long before the asbestos scare; nobody realised just how dangerous it was back then. I wanted to learn how to do suspended ceilings. I was with them for two years and I picked it up very quickly. I was soon doing them on my own, another string to my bow. It wasn't long before I was sub contracting with a lad who fetched and carried for me. I worked all over Sussex, on the Sussex University doing ceilings, several hospitals and several blocks of offices. I did this school in Hastings which had a huge curved ceiling. It was a work of art and it looked fantastic when it was finished. We were asked to do the Tax Office in Brighton. Apparently the office workers were complaining saying that when they shut a door all this fibreglass insulation came through the holes in the tiles and it would fall all over their desks and then apparently over the years the insulation had just disintegrated into dust, it was in a bit of a state. We had to do it on nights. I did not particularly like night work but the money was very attractive. We had to wear protective suits, hats and masks. We took the tiles down, bagged the old fibreglass and replaced the old tiles with new insulation in plastic bags. The dust was so thick you had to change your mask every ten minutes! It was a terrible job, after a week we had had enough and they got another gang of blokes to do it.

CHAPTER NINE

This led to an important part of my life. After we finished this job I developed a tickly cough, I could not shake it off: I had it for weeks, then I started wheezing. I went to the doctor's and he said I had asthma and gave me some puffers which eased it for a while but I was losing my voice and finding it harder to breathe. I went to the doctor again and he told me to go to the hospital. I went up the Sussex County and saw Mr Tranter. He put a camera up my nose and down my throat. He said he would like me to come in for biopsy the next day. I did this. The following day I was sitting on the bed and the Ward Sister came over and told me I had throat cancer. This was very bad timing as it was just before visiting time. In those days the world 'cancer' meant the end. When you got cancer in those days, it was regarded as a death sentence. In those days, nobody ever mentioned the word, it was strictly taboo, in fact it was called the big "C". This was going round in my head when Mags came up with the kids. I couldn't say anything then as I knew it would upset her. I told her to come up that evening on her own as they would let me go home for two days and that I would have to come back. When we got halfway home I pulled over and then I told her. There were floods of tears from both of us. Two days later I was admitted and I was in bed when Mr Tranter came in the ward. He came over to my bed and sat down. He explained to me that we have two vocal chords and that I had a growth on one of mine. He said he would operate that afternoon and then I would have to have a course of radiotherapy. He said it was very unusual for a man of my age to get this. I was only thirty years old at the time.

Learning on Hove Lagoon.

I had the operation with no problem but the radiation at first was a bit daunting. I had to have a perspex face and neck mask made. This had two holes in the neck part. It was then bolted to the table. I was laying on it so that they could direct the laser in the same spot every time. I was very lucky because I was not affected by this even my hair did not fall out like many others. I arranged for my appointments for late in the afternoons and Alan and I would call in to the hospital on the way home from work. I was lucky to make a full recovery. What surprised me was the amount of people in the waiting room having treatment. I got to know Mr Tranter very well, also in later life I called him by his first name Robert (Bob). I did not know at the time but I was his first patient after his move to Brighton. He did say to me if there is anything you want to do then do it, implying that it could come back.

That is what got me into windsurfing. About six months earlier I was down on Hove sea front. The weather was appalling, it was blowing a gale and raining. I loved to see the sea when it was really rough. I was standing on the promenade when this big BMW pulled up and this fella got out. He got this surfboard off the roof and proceeded to put his wetsuit on. I thought he was just going surfing but then he unhooked this sail. It was all new to me. He then rigged it to this frame, all very strange. He then put on this harness, he stood there at the water's edge watching the waves which were as tall as him, one wave broke and rolled up the beach, as it did he held the sail over his head, and ran into the sea. To my amazement he jumped on the board and when the wind hit his sail he shot off like a rocket. When he hit the next wave he was launched into space, ten even fifteen feet high. These days I know the kite surfers do these kind of jumps all the time but in those days I had not seen anything like it! It was so exciting to watch. I found out later he was a professional windsurfer.

Well I thought I've got to have some of that. I joined Hove Lagoon Windsurfing Club and spent many hours falling in and getting many bruises. Their boards were planks compared with today's lightweight boards and their sails were very small and underpowered. Once you had learned to balance and got the thing moving it was great fun. I met two good friends down there and I still see them today, Rob Dewberry and Tony Giles. We were all at the same level and we had so much fun.

Back home having a cuppa.

One time we had all had a good day and a group of six or seven were sitting on the grass bank talking when this dog came over. He walked up to one of the lads and cocked his leg up his back. He turned around and grabbed the dog by its collar and tail and walked it to the water's edge and threw it in. The owner came running over shouting, the lad turned around and said to him, "One word from you and you follow it!"

After a few months we got better and were sailing on the River Adur and the sea. We ventured out when it wasn't too rough. I did have one dodgy moment on the river after a good morning's sailing. We were about to pack up when I fell in, somehow I was under the water and the pressure of the flowing river trapped me between the sail and the boat's mooring rope. I really had to struggle to get out of that one but it was another learning curve.

One thing we all had trouble with was water starting. This was a method of getting back on your board after falling off in deeper water without using the up haul method. This meant climbing on your board and pulling the sail up and grabbing the boom. To water start you virtually sat in the water with the wind on your back, you dragged the boom and the sail over your board lifting the sail at the same time and in one movement let the wind pull your sail dragging you out and onto your board. We were all struggling to do this. Tony told us he was going on a course to learn water starting. One weekend off he went, that weekend the wind got up and Rob and I were down at Hove Lagoon and we kept at it and finally cracked it. When

Tony came back he could not believe it, we were water starting better than him!

One sunny day I was down the lagoon and there were a few learners on the pool. I was watching and yelling a few instructions and I sat on the wall next to this fella. I recognised him, it was Chris Tarrant, his girlfriend was learning on the pool. In the conversation I said I was going to give my kids lessons and I asked him if he got on well with kids; he said he hated them. I thought that it was a strange thing to say as he was presenting Tiswas – a children's programme!

In full flight.

As time went by we all got better, we were learning all the time, and there were never two days the same. I am afraid to say but windsurfing took over my life. If the wind was blowing I was always down the beach, being self-employed I could arrange work around it. I had days when I would try to launch in impossible waves and get myself wrapped around a groin wrecking my gear. I got out one day and I was so pleased when 'Bang!' My mast broke, it was about head high and being made of fibreglass it was jagged and splintered. It hit me in the face and there was blood everywhere mixed with the sea water. It looked like someone had cut my throat. I could see the looks from people watching on the beach, I was very lucky I did not do more damage than I did. I also had some big frights. I had broken one major law… never go out on your own. This afternoon the sun was out and there was a steady force four blowing and I was sailing in and out and I got bored. There was a ship waiting to come in the harbour, anchored about three miles off. I thought I would sail out to it. I was absolutely flying, it was further out than I thought but I was comfortable hooked in and going like the wind. Eventually I reached it and saw it was a large container ship and I could see there was nobody on watch. I sailed across the bow and jibed I then came back across the stern, not a good idea. As I went by the wind around the stern of the ship was causing a vortex and it back winded my sail; in the drink I went. I was about twenty yards from the stern and there was no wind behind the ship but the stern was rising and falling with the waves and the swell. The propeller was huge and it was smashing into the sea. I was slowly getting dragged towards it, I cannot explain how frightened I was. I shouted and whistled but no one could hear me. I was too far out for anyone to see me. I was getting closer and I put in some extra energy from somewhere and I managed to swim and drag my gear away from the stern with an immense struggle. I managed to water start and I sailed in. I'm not religious but when I hit that beach I laid there and thanked God. Afterwards people said, "Why didn't you sit on the board and paddle it to safety?" What they didn't realise was the board I was sailing was a sinker, it floated but not with my weight on it. It worked like a water ski, when it was powered up with the sail it was very quick, also you had more control over it with your feet in the foot straps, you could even jump waves and if you were brave enough you could do forward and backwards loops.

I did have one other bad experience... We had been sailing all day. It was in the afternoon, a really good day for sailing, blowing a force five. There were white horses everywhere, I was always getting a bollocking for going out too far but there were a few lads about so I didn't worry. I was having a great time. When this huge white water wave jacked up in front of me I jumped and I was so high I bottled out. I landed a few feet away from my gear and started to swim towards it. I was quite a strong swimmer but just as I got to it another white wall of water would wash it away and I just could not get to it. In the end I was exhausted, I just had to let it go and swim in. I stopped and looked around and there were no other sailors about. I looked at my watch and it was half past three, the beach looked miles away. It started to get dark and I could see tiny lights flickering on the shore, the sea was still very rough. Luckily the wind was blowing on shore and so I knew I would get washed up on the beach eventually. I was not sure if I would still be alive! I was getting pounded by the waves, I must have swallowed gallons of water. All these things were going through my mind like — will I make it and if I don't what kind of Christmas will the kids have. I was also getting very cold; eventually I felt the sand under my feet and I crawled up the beach, it was seven o'clock!

I must have laid there for a quarter of an hour. I had been washed down a dozen or more beaches. After I had recovered I thought maybe my gear had survived. I walked down about another four beaches and there it was without a mark on it! I picked it up and carried it back to my car. When I got home no one even asked why I was so late getting home. It was absolute paradise under the hot shower. I never told any of my family about my experience.

About this time I quite fancied a camper van, one of my mates had one, Tony Giles. I couldn't afford one so I bought a van and decided to build one myself. Week by week I bought the bits and after about ten weeks I had completed it: white cupboards, white black trim, a double bed which folded up into a seat, spotlights and two tone grey carpets and trim, orange curtains and cushions, a cooker and a fridge. I took all the measurements off of Tony's. I had it quite a time but it was a bit slow so I decided to change the engine for a bigger one. I bought a two litre one, it was a VW so it wasn't a difficult job. The problem was I should have changed the clutch. On the old one it was cable but the bigger engine should have been hydraulic and to push the clutch in was very hard. It really took an effort.

I soon got fed up with that and I flogged it. One of the only motors I have made money on. In 1987 Mags bought a raffle ticket at our local radio station, Southern Sound, and she got the first prize, a brand new Vauxhall Viva, the first time we had a new car and we had it parked on the driveway. I remember the year because one October night we had the big storm, it devastated Sussex, it uprooted many trees and it took walls down and many people lost the tiles off their roofs. Some even lost their roofs! It was quite amazing, we and our neighbours all lost tiles off the roofs. They were scattered all over the garden and the driveway but not one had hit her car.

My mate, Alan, lived just around the corner from me in a very old cottage in the Old Village. At the bottom of the hill was an old factory which once was a brewery. It had a bike shed to park about eight bikes, this was all made of iron. The wind had picked it up and dumped it straight through Alan's roof.

The following day Rob and I went down to Weymouth for the windsurfing speed trials. We were both sailing and that was another magic day sailing. I did try to get the kids interested, I got them lessons but none of them were interested.

I did have a week away in Fuerteventura with the lads. We were all staying in a place called Corralejo, we had rented this place on the beach. We hired a couple of motors which were real wrecks but they got us all over the island. There were eight of us and in those days you didn't have to pay for your gear. You can imagine what it looked like, we all had two boards, mast, booms, and about three sails each. When we left the airport we had all this gear strapped on the roof rack and we all had large bags for our clothes and our wetsuits and harnesses and stuff. One of the lads had been there before and he said we should also take a roof rack with us because you could not get one there. The cars we had were only little Vivas and the stuff was piled on the roof about three foot high. It was well worth the effort though, it was sun, sand, clear water and wind.

The locals told us to be careful of the sharks. We thought that they were winding us up but the next morning we went down the beach and washed up there was a six foot shark. It was very good for our water starts as you didn't want to stay in the water very long!

In the bay was an island called Lobos. Well one day we thought we would sail over to it and climb to the top. There wasn't much wind that morning and so we rigged the largest sail we had and off we went. We got there in about half an hour and we tried to climb to the top. It was impossible because it was made up of little balls of volcanic lava. We were larking about for about three or four hours and we hadn't noticed the wind had got up and was blowing quite hard. We knew we would have trouble getting back. You could not reef a sail on a wind surfer and make it smaller, we got flattened so many times but we got back eventually much to our relief. I also remember some of us had gone to the bottom end of the island where they do the speed sailing and we had a go. The wind blew from the North and offshore, the water was very flat and shallow, it was good fun. I was sitting on the beach watching some of the lads, I was looking at Rob and he was coming to a halt when he stepped off his board. He jumped and yelled, he had stepped on a huge ray which lifted him out of the water. That was talked about for a very long time after that. Rob was quite a big guy but he came up that beach like a long dog. They were good memories.

CHAPTER TEN

One time we were working up in Croydon with half a dozen blokes and we had our lunch on the balcony. It was in the summer and Colin, the paper hanger, was giving us a bit of lip. We were about five floors up, Keith Addison noticed that there was a hairdresser opposite and he said that Colin would get his hair cut at dinnertime.

At one o'clock, he went and we were having lunch when Keith noticed the shop had the phone number on the front and Keith picked up the phone and said to the receptionist that he was calling from a home up the road; he said one of our patients had got out and was seen going in the shop. He said he was dressed in white overalls and a red shirt. He said he was not dangerous but could they keep hold of him until he came and picked him up. Eventually, he convinced them that he was working over the road and they finally let him go. Keith was a big wind-up-merchant. I got him back eventually. One day we had this job to do again in Croydon. We had to build about ten new offices on the top floor. It was quite a big open space with a small door in the corner. Well, Keith had this habit of having a tom tit as soon as we arrived on the site. He went in the toilet and as I went in for a pee, I noticed there was a row of cubicles, about five in number. I went into the big room and being a nosy git, I had a look in a cupboard and it had all the plumbing for the toilets. I dived in and pulled all five levers to flush the toilets and I rushed up to the other end of the room where all the lads were sitting having a cup of tea. A few minutes later, Keith came in and he was fuming. He said he was sitting there and the toilet flushed and caught him out and he ended up with wet pants. One of the lads said you had to be quick because it was automatic and it flushed after a certain time. Nobody told Keith and every morning for four weeks I did the same thing and none of the lads said anything.

One morning, the governor turned up and he called Keith and I over. He said could we build a partition in the toilets. Keith said to the boss, don't talk to me about toilets, that automatic flushing is a right pain in the arse. The governor and the architects looked at him like he was mad. I was standing behind Keith and I mouthed to the others not to say anything; they were cracking up and laughing. Anyway, I told Keith a couple of years ago.

Keith and myself have done some amazing jobs. We subcontracted for a firm called KD Partitions and one of the biggest jobs we did was a partition in a new B&Q. It divided up this huge building in two. We built it with jumbo stud. It was over thirty feet tall and we then had to cover it both sides with two layers of half-inch plasterboard. We had a forklift and a flying carpet to work with, as well as a tower scaffold. I was working at the top of the tower with Beck when he accidentally knocked a pump screwdriver off the top. A pump screwdriver is about two feet long, made of metal with a point at one end and a wooden handle on the other. I shouted below, but this startled Keith and he looked up and the screwdriver hit him straight between the eyes. Luckily, it hit him with the handle end he had a super black eye but it could have been really nasty.

Another time I was struggling to push a plasterboard between the wall and the purlin. Beck said, "No problem," and swiftly shinned down the scaffold and two minutes later he was back up with a lump of old pallet about three foot long. He pushed the end between the purlin and the stud. He managed to prise it apart and I slid the plasterboard in. But then there was an almighty crack: it had snapped and Beck had disappeared and I was too frightened to look over the edge. But somehow he managed to grab the scaffold and was on the platform below. It was an amazing escape.

It could be a dangerous place, a building site. On our way to London, we passed a building site in Brixton. It was a block of flats, a skeleton site with no walls. One day, they were loading up with sand there was a huge pile and I remarked to Keith how big the pile was. The following day, the road was cordoned off and there were police everywhere. Apparently, what happened was it had rained in the night and the sand had doubled its weight and the floor had given way and two labourers were underneath and were both killed.

After the IRA had finished destroying what they could in London, we had a lot of ceilings to repair. We could be three or four streets away from the explosion yet the windows would be blown in and the pressure would lift the suspended ceilings about a foot, and when they came down they would snap the wires that held them up. One lunchtime, Keith and I went for a walk to where the bombs went off; the devastation was incredible. The streets were covered in glass and papers and as you looked up at the blocks of offices, all the blinds were flapping in the wind. It was terrible and is something that sticks in my mind and always will.

Keith and I also did a stint in Hull; that was a long old drive. We would drive up on Monday mornings and come home on Fridays. We found a lovely digs to stay at all week. It was clean and tidy and the landlady was a dream: long blond hair, nice figure and in her thirties. When all the lads went up the pub after work I would often stay at the digs. The lads couldn't understand why I got an extra sausage or a bit of extra bacon on my breakfast or why I got a larger dinner. As I said, she was a lovely landlady and very obliging. She actually said to me that she felt guilty taking my money. You can use your imagination for the rest.

We did have a short stint in Saudi Arabia but that all went tits up. When we met the agent to pick up the tickets, he tried to persuade us to take a couple of bottles of spirits for him — don't worry, they never check your bags, he said. We didn't fancy time in a Saudi jail and we refused point blank. We got on the plane — a jumbo jet, it was one of Air Saudi's — no complaints there; plenty to eat and drink. But when we landed at Kuwait, it was very late in the evening, about eleven, I think, I stepped off the plane and the heat hit me, it was like someone holding a fire close to my face. I thought, blimey, I've made a mistake here! Anyway, we went through customs and I thought I'll take some snaps. I went to my bag and the camera had gone. It wasn't until later that I found out my expensive sunglasses had also gone. A great start.

We were picked up and taken to a very posh hotel. After we had got cleaned up, we went down and had a bit of lunch. Keith got up and asked if I would like a scotch. Ha! Ha! All alcohol free.

The next morning, I could not believe what happened. The noise that woke me was someone mowing the grass. I expected sand as far as the eye could see, but it was all built up with offices with lawns. We got a phone call to say that they would pick us up later in the afternoon and so it gave us a chance to have a bit of a look around. There were bazaars, all dark and full to the brim with carpets, clothing and brass and silver stuff. The men would sit around smoking their hookah pipes. The pavements were red where they chewed these nuts and spat on the ground. The women were not allowed in front of their pick-ups and had to sit in the back. The other thing you could not help noticing was very few women wore shoes and they had the ugliest feet in the world.

We went back to the hotel, collected our bags and tools and went down to the reception about half past three. This limo pulled up and we put our bags in the boot. We sat in the back and off we went. It was not long before we got out of the centre of Kuwait that the houses made of brick or concrete got very sparse and the further you got out of town, the worse it got. The houses were built of anything they could get their hands on: old sheets of ply and corrugated iron. And then there was sand; so much sand it went on forever. The road was concrete, four lanes and illuminated and bright as a day. We did come across the old wreck of a motor. At one point we passed this dead carcass of a camel. Not a pretty sight.

The driver turned around and asked us if we wanted a coffee. We said yes and he passed over these two tiny cups with this thick black stuff in them. It was foul. Keith drunk his and mine, as well. Eventually, we reached the border and we stopped. This bloke came out, he looked like a general in the army. As he was checking our papers, I looked down and there was this old man squatting on his haunches. He looked up at me and smiled and every tooth in his head was made of gold, they were like a row of tombstones.

We were waved through and finally we reached the site. We were welcomed by many people and must have shaken a dozen hands. We were sat down and given a slap-up meal. After that, we were shown where we would be staying. There was a row of Nissen huts and we were both in the first left bedroom. There were two beds and a little wardrobe. There was a long corridor leading down to the washhouse and the toilets. It was adequate. We crashed out; it had been a long day.

Next morning, we were up with the lark. This arab came around to show us the ropes. First, we had a pick-up truck and then they gave us six Pakistani labourers, and then they took us down to the site. It was quite a way away down an unmade road, huge great bumps and potholes. When we got to the site I was amazed. All these brand new tools were left lying about. The thought of having your hands cut off was a good deterrent against pinching anything.

The actual site was run by the Yanks. We were supposed to be building a port ready for a new town they were going to build. I say 'supposed' because we could do nothing: there was no materials at all. Just a few bits and pieces. It was very difficult to stand around and do nothing, we had to be on site from eight until five and the heat up in the eighties.

Because everything was new, it was quite exciting. At the end of the day, a hooter would sound and all the Pakistanis would come out of the woodwork and run to get a lift in the back of the pick-up truck. We drove back to where we were the previous evening and sat down for a meal. When they brought it to us, it was foul and inedible. Keith was not amused and we both complained and we both refused to eat it. The smell was something like an old dustbin. We did rant on a bit and eventually they took us to the American's food hall. We went in and they made us very welcome and they said, "Help yourselves to anything." Well, I had never seen anything like it. There were two tables about thirty feet long with every kind of salad, roast meat, sweets and fruit. Oh! And a soft ice cream machine. It was heaven. As you can imagine, we ate there all the time after that. We did try to move into the American quarters but they wouldn't wear it. We kept on asking about materials and they kept on saying it was on a ship somewhere.

One day, while wandering around the site, we came across two plasterers who were doing some tyraling: a process of stippling a wall. It was a hand-held sort of tray, you turned a handle and it flicked this stuff on the wall. Anyway, this big black American came along and was watching what the spread's were doing.

He said, "What a fantastic machine."

I replied, "Of course, it was made in England!"

He thought for a minute and in a slow southern drawl he said, "Bull shit."

We all cracked up.

Another time, we were mooching around when all of a sudden this hooter went, the sky turned orange and everyone seemed to disappear. Then all of a sudden, it went quite dark. Then it hit us: a sand storm. We crouched down behind a wall. Then we tried to get to a different part of the building. We only had on shorts, a T-shirt, and boots and it was really painful, like standing in a sand blaster. It blew for about half an hour and then it went as quick as it came. Nobody told us what to expect.

Saudi was a strange place to work, not that we did much. We were apparently building a port for all the stuff to come into to build a new town. It was a huge site. I remember that it was all run by the American army and one day, we had a visit from a five-star general. The preparation for this visit was amazing. All the Pakistanis and Filipinos spent all of two days just sweeping up the sand inside the buildings and laying strips of carpet. Although it was a nice, alcohol-free country, there was a crate of lager on every corner. All the labourers were told to have the day off and not to be seen.

When he arrived, he had a limo with American flags flying on both wings; even the number plate was blue with five gold stars on it. There was a lot of saluting and hand shaking with the Arabs. He wandered around for about an hour and vanished as quick as he had arrived. We did manage to swipe a couple of beers but the rest just vanished. How anything got finished I do not know. It was a crazy place.

They were pumping wet concrete in through the roof of this corridor and there were about a dozen Pakistanis trying to lay this floor and dodge the concrete. When a truck pulled up at the door and these Americans threw half a dozen pairs of wellingtons, it was a free-for-all; some were rolling in the wet concrete. When it all calmed down, some only had one wellington boot.

Another time, we saw about six blokes sitting around in a circle and when we went over we could see they were trying to dig a hole for a lamppost. They were only using their hands and as quick as they pulled it out, it went back in. Unbelievably, at the end of the day, there it was, this lamppost all done.

Some of their technology was amazing. One day, when we were wandering about, we watched these four huge great lorries. They were in formation. They were in a huge circle, all facing the same way. On the backs of these lorries, they were all supporting one huge steel circle about eight feet high. The drivers were all on their walkie-talkies and they were trundling down to the site. When they got there, three huge cranes met them hitched up to this circle of steel and lifted it onto of several others. We asked what it was and we were told it was a section of a huge silo which would store cement.

I think I mentioned before that at the end of the day, all of our Pakistani labourers would appear and get in the back of the pick-up truck. Well, all of the lads, and I am afraid to say including myself, would put our foot down on the unmade road and see how many we could lose off the back. They weren't treated very well and we were under strict instructions not to take out any food for them, but we would smuggle out the odd orange, apple or banana. We got quite friendly with the one who seemed to be their foreman and if we ever were stood still chatting, one would appear with a chair.

One of the Pakistanis who worked in the office was well educated and spoke very good English. One day, he broke his ankle and we took him to our doctor and he bandaged him up. The following day, we got such a bollocking: they were not allowed to see our doctors.

He made us chuckle one day when we were leaving. He asked if he could have something to remember us by. He said any small memento would do. We had nothing to give him and so I got my wallet out and started looking through it. I came across a stamp, which he said would be fine. He pointed at it and said: "Queen Elizabeth Taylor!"

After about six weeks, Keith and I had had enough. We had to be on site all day and the materials had not arrived and so there was nothing to do. We had seen everything and we were bored to tears. And so, we decided we were going home. We were taken in front of the big bosses (Arabs) and we said we were going. They said that we can't and that they would give us more money. We said, no thanks and they said, we haven't said how much. We told them that it didn't matter how much because we were going home. They could not believe it: they thought they could buy anything or anybody.

The next day, we got all our stuff together and got a lift to the Saudi border. There was another lad with us. They let us through the Saudi border but then there was about three hundred yards of no-man's land. We got walking and got to the Kuwait border control and they would not let us in. We walked back to the Saudi border and they would not let us back in. The guards got quite aggressive and so we tramped back to the Kuwait border.

By this time, we were getting quite worried. They still would not let us in. We sat down on our bags with our heads in our hands. Then this lad who was with us said that he had an idea. He got up and went to the office and the next we knew, he beckoned us through. We picked up our bags and ran. We caught up with him and he said that he had told the guard he had a phone call and his wife was expecting and she was about to give birth. Apparently, the guard was a father of nine and was quite sympathetic. We got a taxi back to the hotel and next day we went to the airport and got on a plane. When we got to Heathrow, we came straight home.

After we got back from Saudi we got a job with KD's again. In those days there was plenty of work about and I did a few ceilings and a bit of dry lining and Keith and I went our separate ways. A couple of weeks later, I bumped into him in Shoreham and he said he was trying to get hold of me as he had got hold of a lot of work in Belgium. He said the money was good. I said I would give it a go and he said, "Right, I'll pick you up at four Monday morning; bring your tools and your passport." I was used to these early starts.

He arrived dead on time. We got in the car and drove along the coast to Dover. (The motorway wasn't built then.) We got our tickets and boarded the ferry. It was a strange feeling like we were quite important or special. There was usually a special reason to go abroad. We bought our fags and drink and had a big fry-up. By that time, we had reached Calais. We drove through France and soon arrived in Brussels. We then drove straight to the site which was huge. I remember ten or twelve blocks of flats; there was acres of metal stud work to do. By eleven a.m. we were working.

We stayed in an old caravan. I remember it was so cold that when I woke up I had to scrape the ice off the inside of the windows. That year, it was so cold even the canals were frozen. We got up, made a cup of tea and had a fag or two. We smoked like troopers in those days. We also worked bloody hard. After work we would get cleaned up and go down to the local restaurant to have a slap-up meal and then pop in the local pub. We would then wander back to the caravan and get our heads down ready for the next day. It soon warmed up and it got quite enjoyable.

We had many laughs. The biggest one was the toilets: the first one was just a shed with a big hole dug in the ground with one bar of wood across it for you to perch on. One of our lads dropped his wallet down the hole and there was no way he was going to retrieve it; the smell was too overpowering. And so the English boys built a new one with a door, a proper seat and we put chemicals in it to take the odour away but in the end that got in a state. One Sunday, some of the lads tipped a gallon of petrol down the hole and a trail about twenty yards away; they put a match to it and blew it into oblivion. The explosion was so loud that someone phoned the law but everyone denied everything. But then we had to build another loo.

The actual method of building in Belgium was completely alien to me: they didn't use scaffolding, their brickwork was done overhand, health and safety was non-existent at first but they did bring it in later.

There was always a crane. The most dangerous thing was that they made these huge wooden platforms and a crane would then lift them up to an opening in the side of the building. They would then swing them in and then when it was halfway in they would hammer a couple of props in the end that was in the room. It was cantilevered with about ten feet overhanging the edge. These were then loaded with materials and you carried them in. When they loaded a stack of our plasterboards, the platform would bend and creak, because we would carry a pair of plasterboards between us before one of us would have to go out to the far end. You guessed right: it was always me. When you were five or six storeys up, it was quite hairy. No hand rails. After a couple of years, they did bring in hard hats and steel toecaps.

A few weeks later I remember they collared Keith's dad. They said he was not wearing steel toecaps. He took his shoes and socks off to reveal that he had no toes: he had lost them to frostbite in the war. They were gobsmacked and they never bothered him again.

We had this Belgian guy whose name was Splatz. He would check our work and generally sort things out. Keith and I had been working on this huge wall. It was a jumbo metal stud and two thicknesses of plasterboards. We had got up to about the fourth floor and this wall was right around the staircase. He said it didn't look right. He cut a long batten and it fitted at the back but when he brought it to the front it was five inches out. Keith and I knew straightaway what had happened. We had fixed the track the wrong side of the line. It was a monster job to take it all down and move.

We waited until Splatz had gone and we came up with an idea. We found an ackrow which is a huge jack for holding up ceilings. We laid it on the floor, braced the other end and started winding. The wall moved over a treat. In the morning, Splatz turned up and he could not figure out how we had dismantled and rebuilt it in the time we had. We never told him. He kept walking about muttering, "It's not possible, it's not possible."

One day we were working and two ladies turned up: Pauline and Rose. They were sisters who originally came from the West End of London. They asked if we needed any digs and we said we would have a look. After work, we got in the car and went round to see what was what. Apparently, they both had houses in the same street about one hundred and fifty yards apart. They said we could use Pauline's and she would move in to her sister's. They also said they would come up the hill early and cook breakfast and light the fire and that they would do us an evening meal as well. We agreed a price and the following Monday we moved in. After the caravan, it was magic. We had our own room and the food was out of this world.

I remember one evening we had another mate with us (Gregg Guile). He was a jointer and we needed him. Anyway, we had got cleaned up and were sitting down ready for the evening meal and Pauline got this steak and kidney pie out of the oven and plonked it on the table. I started to divide it in to three when she said, "No, you have got one each."

I even remember going home one weekend and Mags saying," I have got you a special for dinner." I could not tell her that I had had steak three times that week already. Apparently, it was quite cheap out there; it was probably horse but it tasted so good and we ate it.

Talking about Gregg, one evening we took him to Brussels and said we would show him the red light area. He was quite a few years younger than us and a bit naive. The area we took him to had all the girls sitting in the windows all looking very attractive in their flimsy clothes. His eyes were like saucers. As we were walking down the road, we stopped outside this place and I shoved Gregg in and we held the door shut. After a few minutes, we let him out: his first visit to a brothel and he came out as white as a sheet. Gregg was a really good mate to go out with because he was a double for George Best and he had no trouble pulling the birds.

He worked with us for a few weeks and then Keith's brothers were on the scene. There was one problem with this: Keith and Brian would argue like cat and dog and even sometimes end up with the pair of them fighting. Brian even tried to push Keith over the side of the stairwell which was a fifty to sixty foot drop. By the end of the day, they would end up talking as if nothing had happened.

I loved working in Belgium; we travelled all over and I saw so many different places. We climbed to the top of the Atomium in Brussels. It felt good to be driving on the other side of the road; it was very enjoyable. I did struggle with the French language and in fact, even after four years, I had learned very little. Everybody wanted to speak in English.

The girls would often sit with us in the evenings and tell us tales about the war and what it was like to live in an occupied country. All over the country are these monuments at the side of the road and we asked them about the one by the side of the canal around the corner. They told us that when the Brits were advancing, liberating the country, there were three British soldiers on a motorbike and sidecar and they were coming along the towpath but as they came around the bend there was a German armed car and they pushed them in the canal. As they were trying not to drown, the Germans shot them. Their names were on the monument.

Pauline had two sons. They were called Arthur and Oscar. Being the eldest, Oscar was just learning to speak when the country was occupied by the Germans and so the girls could only talk to him in French and so his English was very limited.

Arthur on the other hand was learning to speak after Belgium was liberated and so the girls talked to him in English and French. He ended up a teacher and a professor of languages whereas Oscar worked in the steel mill in the town.

One morning, we could hear this commotion going on outside. Well, when we went to work, we could see the whole front of the house next door was covered in mauve drapes except for the front door which was open. We looked in but it was very dark. Someone asked if we would like to have a look and being nosey, Keith and I went in. It was a very long passage and when we got to the end someone put the hall light on and up the end was a coffin stood up against the end wall with the old boy in it. We made a quick retreat: not something you see every day.

While we were working there, Oscar was building another storey on top of his bungalow. There were no health and safety or building regulations. If you wanted another floor, you built it; if it fell down, it was your own fault. They asked us to do the plasterboarding for him. We agreed but when we arrived, we could hardly believe our eyes. The roof was practically built with dismantled pallets. The walls were built with one skin of blocks; no cavity or insulation. I asked if anyone had checked the footings to see if they could take any extra weight. The answer was a shake of the head.

One evening, I could see Oscar's wife on her hands and knees in the back garden. I later found out what she was doing. She was digging a trench with a hand trowel; it was about six inches wide and nine inches deep. This was to take away the waste from the second bathroom. The trench made the pipe, which was made of plastic, about four inches under the surface which was then connected to a cesspit. I think it was lucky the lawn had a slope running away from the house otherwise it would never have run away. The thing is, when they were finished they looked fantastic. It was just the construction that let them down.

As I said, Arthur was a school teacher and he asked me if my son, Paul, would like to go with him and a group of lads down to the Ardennes. He went and I thought it was very brave of him. He spoke no French and to go away for a week really surprised me. But he thoroughly enjoyed it.

One day, the girls said, "We will take you to Ronquer." We asked what this was and they said we would have to wait and see. We arrived after about a quarter of an hour and what greeted us was simply amazing. Although we think of Belgium as being as flat as a witch's tit there was this huge hill. The canal was level at the bottom and the other canal was level at the top. What happened was there was a huge tank with forty or fifty wheels and it was angled at the bottom so the top was level. They were like railway lines going up the hill and they would bring it to the bottom and like a lock they would fill it with water. Then they opened the gates and the barge would float in and they would shut the gates and this monster machine would thunder up the hill and they would open the gates the other end, and off the barge would go. There were two of these huge machines and as one went up, one came down. It was work of mechanical genius. I hope I've explained it; it was something quite amazing.

When we arrived on a new site, I would go in the site office and find out what we had to do. The foreman always had a couple of crates of beer and he said we could help ourselves. Keith would get quite annoyed because I wouldn't tell him until the job was almost finished. It never bothered me. I could take it or leave it. I was more of a scotch drinker myself. Keith would drink anything as long as it was alcoholic.

One winter we were working in this bungalow, putting the ceilings up. The canals had ice on them and there was snow on the ground. There were no windows in this place and it was bloody freezing. We were about halfway through when the owner turned up. He went to the boot of his car and produced a bottle of scotch. We thanked him and off he went. Keith and I had a sip and then another and before we knew it, the whole bottle had gone. It did the job because we felt nice and warm and we still drove home.

In most of the lay-bys there was a van selling sausages and chips (fricadelle and frites). Keith and I had had a hard day and we pulled into one on the way home. We were sitting in the car eating them when all of a sudden the girls pulled in behind us. They had a right go at us for eating that rubbish and spoiling our dinner and we didn't get enough food at home. We were caught banged to rites.

One day, we awoke to this hell of a racket. When we went out of the front, the girls had dragged a full size gas bottle up the cobbled hill. Keith and I took it off them. It was all we could do to lift it. To think the girls were in their mid-seventies; they were amazing, they looked after us like we were their own. After we stopped working in Belgium, I would still keep in touch. I rang regularly and me and my family would often visit and stay for a week.

We were working over there when the farmers were protesting about the sheep imports. We were on our way home on a Friday afternoon when we got caught up in a traffic jam. It was three lanes wide. I was driving so Keith got out and it wasn't very long, just moving very slowly. Keith came back and said it was blocked with tractors which were moving very slow. We stayed there for about half an hour when a Mercedes with a German number plate came down the hard shoulder. They saw him coming and blocked it and then all hell let loose. A lot of people got out of their cars and were running to the front. They were banging his car, kicking it and climbing all over it. Then the drivers started coming back with their trophies. One had the aerial, others came back with the chrome strips and of course the hubcaps. When we finally got down that far he was still locked in what was left of his motor. It was wrecked: four flat tyres and the bodywork was covered in dents. As we drove by, the other drivers were cheering and tooting their horns. All the time that this was happening there were two police cars parked on the bridge over the motorway; they never lifted a finger to help. We did get a bit worried as they kept looking at our number plate and the protest was about the import of British sheep. We finally got past and arrived at Calais about two hours late.

It was at this time that I gave up smoking. I was working on my own in this bungalow. Keith had gone somewhere and I had stopped for a fag. I lit one up and then turned around and I had another one on the go, and when I turned right around I realised I had four fags on the go. I thought, this is crazy. Enough is enough. I stopped, on the spot. I kept a packet in my top pocket and eventually they fell to bits — disintegrated. I kept saying to myself, if I need one, I've got one. But I kept putting it off. I remember I went to a wedding and I was sitting opposite Harry Davis and after the lunch and the champagne (and wine and beer and scotch), he kept saying, "Have a fag, you miserable bastard!" In the end, I gave in and lit one up. Later I was violently sick; I blamed the fag, although it could have been all the booze. Not bad for a thirty to forty-a-day man.

Belgium, unlike what many people would say, is not boring. It's a very beautiful and interesting country. Bruge, for instance, is a fantastic place. As is Waterloo and Brussels. Every year the whole square is covered with a huge picture made up with flowers. It is quite spectacular. I loved the way the funfairs and markets would take over the whole town centre. And everything is so clean and tidy; very little graffiti. The roads were lovely to drive on; no potholes and all illuminated. I sound like a promotion video now so I'll shut up about it. Eventually, after four years, the work dried up and we said cheerio to the girls and we came home.

We had this job to do in Dunsfold. It was where they built the Harrier, the vertical take-off fighter plane. At lunchtimes, we were allowed to just be nosey and wander around. This was very interesting and we saw them assembling planes. I watched them building the ejector seats inside; they resembled the back of a TV. One day, we were working in one of the offices and there was one hell of a crashing sound and I thought one of the planes had crashed. When I looked out, what they were doing was testing the landing gear. It was amazing to see. This plane that costs who knows how many millions, would hover about ten feet up and then they would turn everything off and that was the noise I had heard; it was amazing. The plane could take it so I guess they knew what they were doing.

The other thing that surprised me was the lack of security. We drove our van into the airport, not even a security man at the gates. We did get a rollicking once for taking a shortcut across the runway but generally, nobody bothered us.

After that, we took on a big job at Christ's Hospital, a big college in Horsham. When we got there, it was bigger than we thought. The whole place had not been changed since the Victorian times. The dormitories were one big room with all the beds equally spaced out and one small locker. The beds were cast iron on wooden boards. They were too heavy to move on our own. Our job was to build dozens of little rooms for them. This was done with metal studs and a plasterboard. It was such a big job, we had to employ a few other guys. We were there for months.

One of these blokes was Brian Stammers. He was jointing and he was on top of ten foot scaffold. He was distracted and stepped off the back. He was a bit overweight and it was a hospital job. It turned out he had ruptured his spleen which was a bit dodgy. He was off for a long time with that.

Another couple of lads we met were from the east end of London and we were talking one lunchtime when I said I needed a new tyre for the van. They said they knew someone who could get me one cheap. I said OK. The next morning, when they came in, they opened up their van and there it was, the tyre and wheel. They had gone out and nicked one, I found out later. They would pinch anything to order. They were on the funny fags and they would drive with the top off the adhesive can to smell the fumes.

Another job we were on in Brighton, we had to put a new ceiling up but we had to take the old one down and the quickest way to do this was to cut the wires and let it fall on the ground and clear it up later. We cut all of the supporting wires and started picking up the tiles and grid when I bent over and felt this sharp pain in my right eye. It was bleeding and I could not see out of it. What happened was one of the wires we had cut was standing upright and when I bent over, this had gone into my eye. They rushed me to hospital. They said I could lose the sight in my eye but thank god after three weeks with a black patch and a dressing, they took it off and I could see.

We were working on a block of flats in Brighton when the foreman came rushing up the stairs and said that everyone had to get off-site because of a bomb alert. Apparently, one of the Irish labourers had dug up this old World War One bomb and was cleaning it with a shovel. Everybody ran off-site. The weather was gorgeous and Keith and I went up on the roof and had a drink and a sandwich, and we soaked up the rays. This day, I must have been very tired. We usually had half an hour and then we would go back to work. Well this day, Keith, being the joker he is, didn't wake me. He had gone back to work and then went home. I woke up at about six thirty and everyone had gone home and the whole place was locked up. I was burnt to a cinder and I had to climb over an eight foot fence. I was not amused but Keith thought it was hilarious.

CHAPTER ELEVEN

Over the years, I had had a go at most trades and so I tried my hand at jobbing building again If something came up and I couldn't do it, I would sub it out to someone who could. I quite enjoyed it although getting paid was sometimes a problem. I did a job for some Arabs. It was a big house on the seafront in Hove. I had to build a wall and plaster it to divide a large room. I worked out it would take me two weeks on my own. I would get the materials at trade price and then give him the bill. He was quite happy; there were loads of them living in this house. I worked late into the evening, sometimes not getting home until nine. Anyway, I finished it in just over a week. He was not a happy bunny and he refused to give me my money. I went down there one evening and demanded my cash. I sat down and this house was very dark and I sat there and the door opened and in came about half a dozen big Arabs. They all stood around me and I must admit I was quite frightened. The boss man stepped forward and said he would not pay.

I stood up and said, "That's OK, I'll go and get a policeman. You're breaking the law."

As soon as I mentioned the law, he went in the other room and came out with the money. He very reluctantly thrust it in my hand and I left. Thankfully, he hadn't called my bluff.

Most of my work was on recommendation and sometimes the customers would give me extra because they were pleased with the job that they got. One day, I got a phone call from Keith. He asked me if I could hang doors. I told him I could and he asked me if I was interested in working with him on this new job. It was building partitions in offices. It was clean and dry and there was plenty of work and that was how I got into the best job I ever had. We still had the driving to do but I didn't mind that. I quite liked travelling and meeting new people. We worked in empty buildings and occupied ones. Nobody but nobody could believe just how quickly we put them up. In the morning there would be an empty space and by the time we went home there would be an office complete with door, window, wallpaper, skirting and suspended ceiling with light fittings. We got through a hell of a lot of work and we then employed a few people to help us out.

One I remember was Ken Townsend. A dam good chippy but he was so slow. He would do anything but what he was supposed to do. Keith and I went looking for him and found him making tea for everyone on the site. Another time, he went missing and we eventually found him in the field behind the job. He was photographing bugs and butterflies. He was a lovely man but when he got down to hanging two doors a day he had to go. In comparison, I hung eight a day.

We also employed his brother but he was so laid back he had to go. And then we had Roy. He was also a good chippy. Think he just got fed up with the job and left. We also employed his son but we caught him going through all the office drawers one morning so he had to go. One of the windsurfing lads said he was looking for a job and I gave him a start. He was bloody useless. I think he was with us three days; he was doing something wrong.

He was a big Herbert but I laid into him with a few f***s and he stood there and sobbed and said, "My mum wouldn't like the way you spoke to me."

I took him home in silence and I never saw him again.

Meanwhile, my daughter got married and the feller she married was quite a nice lad called Wayne. The problem was, he worked in a shop and didn't earn a lot of money. Well, he came to work with us. He was very keen and wanted to learn. He ended up working with me for years even after I finished with Keith. At first, he would fetch and carry and was a lot like a young me. He watched and learned and got to be a good fixer. The only thing he couldn't and wouldn't do was hang doors. We would have a competition carrying boards. If I carried two he would carry three and then I would carry four. When we carried panels, I would get one end and he would get the other and I would run. There was plenty of banter but he would never come out on top. He did try.

We subtracted from KD Partitions and we did work all over Sussex and occasionally we did the odd job for Rediffusion at Crawley. It was a huge firm which specialised in building simulators for the airlines. These jobs got more frequent and eventually we were there full time. We were taking down offices and rebuilding new ones and generally refurbishing old ones. We got to know everyone and even had our own photographic passes. And we could go anywhere; any tools that we did not have we just went to the store and got them. We were allowed to have lunch and dinner for free. It was like working direct for them. Every week, someone from KD's would turn up and tell us what to do and bring up the drawings. One Christmas, we were working and most of Rediffusion's men were on holiday and we got chatting to one of the fellas and he asked if we would like a go in the simulator. We said, yes please, and went aboard. It was a cabin of seven four seven perfect in every detail. They explained it was even better than a real plane, it had to simulate things that could go wrong like an engine fire or decompression in the cabin. The screen could be changed to any airport day and night or rain. The amazing part was that when you sat in the chair and it started moving you could not believe you were not in the plane. I almost gave myself a heart attack crashing a seven-four-seven in Dubai. It was quite an experience and was something I could not stop talking about.

In those days, computers were huge and the main one filled a whole room. That was when I fitted my first false floor. That was another fantastic job. The floor was made from two inch thick by two foot squares covered with steel plate and a carpet tile on the top. We had to cut them with a band saw. These were supported on adjustable steel legs. In the end, most of the offices had these floors.

This computer room was a dodgy place to work. If there was a fire, the whole room filled with alon gas which could kill a person in minutes. Alon gas puts out fires without damaging the computers. Of course, it's banned now. There were quite a lot of laughs too. We were building a new boardroom and every day when we finished somebody would come around and say they didn't like this or that and we would have to take it down and re-do it again and many of the workers would see this when they came in in the morning. They would always comment on it. In the end, I had a board made up with Yo-Yo Partitions on it which raised a smile or two.

I almost forgot to tell you about the bottle game. It was something I picked up in Belgium. We were in this bar and I could hear this commotion going on in another bar. Being nosey, I had a look and there was a crowd of people betting on these two fellas. One at a time they would toe the line and then they would, holding a half pint bottle in each hand, walk out on the bottles and they would leave one there and come back on the other without your hands touching the floor. The one who left it out the furthest was the winner. I thought I'd have a go. Well, I was rubbish. But after a few weeks of practising I developed a technique. I had very long arms and very strong tummy muscles due to my ceiling work and windsurfing.

Now for some not so good memories, and some great memories. We had this big concrete shed outside in the back garden and I thought I would make it into an office. I dry lined it, fitted a new window and door and a suspended ceiling. It was summer time and I left the front door open as I would often get mates pop in for a cup of tea. All the lads did this. I was working out the back when one of the lads did pop in, it was Mad Mel. He got his name because he had no fear. He came straight in and out the back and I said to him, give Mags a shout and she will make us a brew. He went in and came back and said she wasn't there. I said she is probably upstairs, give her another shout. He did this and got no reply. I said don't worry I will make you one. I walked in the kitchen and I saw on the worktop there were four notes each with a name on it, Graham, Karen, Paul and myself. Before I opened my note I somehow knew what it said… that she had left us. There was a lot of tears shed that night when it had sunk in and for a few weeks after that. They say forgive and forget but I can still visualise those kids after she went. I still see her now but I find it very difficult. I am very easy going and I don't want to upset the apple cart so I accept things as they are, all the kids accept her now that they are grown up and two of them have children.

When she went Karen was sixteen, I think Paul had left home a year earlier. I think Karen grew up very quick, she stood no nonsense from anybody and she ran the house. I know I paid the bills but she organised everything. I worked my butt off to pay off the outstanding bills and there were plenty of those! She had been to Brighton Secretarial

College and had a job at Lloyds Bank; she had her head screwed on.

There were a lot of memories in that house and reminders of better times. I did get someone to follow Mags and I subsequently found out she had left me for another bloke who she had met when she went to Ten Pin Bowling. I suppose I should have seen it coming, but as they say you're always the last to know. There was no alternative thought, when Mags was out in the evenings I got very friendly with my neighbour over the road, Jenny, because her husband went down the pub to play darts on the same nights that Mags went bowling. We both had a lot in common and we both liked Scotch; sometimes she would bring a bottle over or sometimes we would drink mine. We had some lovely evenings.

Shortly after that her husband took over the pub in the Old Village so that romance faded but we still kept in touch. My son, Graham, was good friends with her son, Paul, and one day he told me she had had a stroke and was paralysed down one side and had lost her speech and could not talk. She moved to a block of flats in Hove and I did pop in and see her a couple of times but now I can't manage the stairs.

I did for a while join a Lonely Hearts Club. I met some sad lonely and desperate women but nothing ever clicked. All of my mates had partners and we did these coach trips to France, Belgium, Holland and Germany. These were great fun, we had a lot of laughs but deep down I hated being on my own.

I was still sailing and having fun and some of my sailing friends were having a party and I got an invitation. I was in two minds whether to go but I'm so glad that I did because I met Jackie. I was standing in the lounge listening to the music and drinking a Scotch when one of the lads came over, Chris Bear, and said to me, "That girl over there with my wife is on her own, her husband has just pissed off and left her."

Jackie, catching some rays.

I looked over and she was stunning, a great figure and really nice face. She smiled and that was that. I got her a drink and we chatted. I asked if she could jive and she said, "Yes."

She had a lovely smile and such an infectious laugh. We chatted and laughed most of the evening. Like me her husband had cleared off with another woman and she didn't want to go to the party either. We agreed to meet again for a drink and I went to her place in Wick, Littlehampton, and we went to this little pub not far from where she lived. We sat and talked for hours, we had so much in common and she even had a daughter the same age as my Karen and when they met they got on like a house on fire. They would go out together and would often come home a bit tipsy. Jackie and I carried on seeing each other and she would often do me dinner. About two weeks later I remember vividly she took me by the hand and led me upstairs. The rest you will have to use your imagination as she could be reading this and is bound to pick me up on something later!

I was still windsurfing and when my fiftieth birthday came around, as I remember, it was a weekend and I was sailing all day.

Come the evening, Karen said, "Can you drop me off at Mile Oak." Jackie was out so I agreed. I dropped her off and she went in then she came running out and said an old friend wanted a word with me. So I parked up and went in and I was greeted by over one hundred of my friends and relatives. Jackie and Karen had arranged everything and I knew nothing. Half the lads I had been sailing with all day knew and they said nothing. It was a great evening with a bar and disco.

The trouble was, back to the bottle game, every time we saw a game on, Keith would enter me and we would win a bit of money. What reminded me of that was at lunchtimes at Rediffusion, I would get some of the office blokes having a go. One day this bloke came in and he wasn't much smaller than seven foot and he said he wanted to give it a try. They were all cheering and he was doing very well. He got as far as me but he couldn't get back without touching the floor. I sighed with relief. In the end, I had to stop because half the staff of Rediffusion would turn up.

CHAPTER TWELVE

That was a good part of my life. All good things have to come to an end and Rediffusion sold out to a French firm called Thomsons and everything changed. For a start, they did more military stuff and small simulators for funfairs and exhibitions. It was quite interesting but it was not the same. We built one screen which was over forty foot long which was used for training army snipers. There were also simulators for learner drivers and Formula One racing cars. Later, we noticed there were different gangs of fixers around the place and our work got less and less. Eventually, KD's lost the contract.

We did a few jobs for KD's. The work got a bit thin on the ground and we were told about a firm in Eastbourne who needed fixers, Sovereign. I gave them a ring and they arranged to meet. They seemed very nice and professional and so we started sub-contracting for them. They were a good firm to work for; good work and good money and they always paid on the dot. Their jobs were nearly all quality. One we did was in the fire station of the channel tunnel. That was very interesting. On one wall there was a very big screen and if there was a person or a fire anywhere in the tunnel they could pan in and see what the problem was. And Sovereign didn't want blood like KD's.

I was still windsurfing when I could and I was getting more proficient. I tried a couple of competitions but soon realised I was not good enough for that. I still knew Nick and Ant and Herby Baker. Nick, by then, was number four in the world and number one in the indoor competitions. He got us some free complimentary tickets and a couple of rooms in a hotel in Paris. We found the venue and we were surprised to find the seats were in the VIP area with tables and drinks. I had never seen an indoor competition before.

Nick racing in Paris.

It was in the centre of Paris; a huge arena with tiered seats. In the centre was a large pool with about twenty huge fans down one side. The whole pool was covered in thousands of balloons. It was sponsored by Swatch and there was a huge watch at one end. At the other end, furthest away from us, were four slopes which ran down to the water. There was piped music and when it stopped there was a countdown. Three. Two. One. And then the fans started up and all the balloons were blown into the audience and were immediately burst. The noise was horrendous. There were balloons everywhere.

When the popping finally stopped, the racing began. They lined up four at a time and the last two were eliminated. It was quite exciting. It was a course of a figure of eight and there were loads of collisions. Anyway, Nick won and then there was a break and then they put this ramp in the water. It had a slot up the centre and it was a work of art to position your board so that the fin at the back would fit in the slot and they would do forwards and backwards loops. Many crashed and broke off their fins. At the end of the day, Nick was crowned champion. After the racing and jumps there was the presentations. Nick got his cheque and two huge great silver cups.

I was helping him put his gear away, he said, "Brian, can you put these cups in the car."

I said, "Of course."

I carried them out of the tunnel and to the car park and the fans, about eighty of them, were cheering and crowding around me. They must have thought I was Nick.

I had quite a few interesting times with Nick. He had bought a flat on the beach and I was doing it up for him.

He said, "I have some help for you this morning.

I knew he was dating a page three girl. But I went into the lounge and there were two page three girls dressed in T-shirts and the tiniest of shorts you ever saw. They were stripping the wallpaper; they were bending over and bouncing up and down. I stayed in the room about a quarter of an hour, but being young and healthy I had to find another job to do. Fascinating, but too much for me.

Another time, I went to call for Nick and he went to get ready and make a cup of tea when his girlfriend came in the room.

She said, "Hello, Brian," and then she said, "I've just had a boob job," and promptly pulled up her top and she was braless. Then she said, "What do you think of them?" and then she virtually shoved them to my face. Well, I'm not a prude but it was a bit of shock.

Nick came in and said, "They look good, don't they?"

I agreed and we carried on as usual.

For a couple of years I carried on doing what I fancied, sometimes working on partitions and ceilings, sometimes jobbing building. I know I never advertised for work; it always found me. I hoped I gave a good job for the right money.

When Mags left, she actually left me with a lot of debt. That's when Karen was a star. I worked extra hard and managed to pay them off. There was an awful lot of memories in that house and I asked the kids if they fancied moving and they agreed and I found this lovely house on the beach at Shoreham, end of terrace with a nice garage and a large driveway and a small garden. It was ideal for my windsurfing. I would be able to rig up in the garden and carry it around the corner to the beach. I took the kids to have a look and they loved it because they could all park on the drive.

Well, Mags' brother was a mortgage broker and I gave him a bell and asked if it was possible. The next day, he rang and told me if I had left it another two weeks the house would be repossessed. That came as a huge surprise. With Karen and Jackie's help, I got square and put the house up for sale. I had one feller who was very interested. Dead keen, he came and looked at it several times and we shook hands on it and the sold sign went up. The kids and I started packing and everything we had was in tea chests. I had hired a skip and there was a family who had just moved in up the road and as fast as I put stuff in the skip, they were taking it out.

We got a day to exchange contracts and the day soon came around. We were all ready to go when I got a phone call and he had pulled out. We were really pissed off. The house went back on the market and we started unpacking. A couple of weeks later I bumped into the guy in Tesco's. I felt like thumping him but I smiled and asked how he was and he said the house he was going to buy fell through and he asked if mine was still for sale. I wanted to say no but a sale is a sale and eventually he bought it and I'm glad to say that it wasn't long after that house prices plummeted.

Jackie and I absolutely loved living on the beach. We would walk for miles on the sand. (How I miss that now.) The first thing I did was to rip out the heating. It was a hot air blower. It was either too hot or too cold. Because it was heated by gas I was also concerned about fumes. I had a friend who helped me put in a completely new central heating unit. The cupboard that held the main unit I turned into somewhere to put your coats. There was a small opening between the lounge and the back room and I changed it to a keyhole entry; very modern in those days. The lounge had no focal point and so I built a false fireplace. When I finished, it looked a picture.

As I have said before, sometimes I would stay at Jackie's place and sometimes she would stay at mine. This weekend I was staying at hers. We came home on a Sunday afternoon to be greeted by the next door neighbour. He said, "Go in, but don't touch anything."

When we went in, our hearts sank. We had been burgled. They had been very professional: taken everything that was worth money. They had even unscrewed my stereo speakers off the walls. They had taken my telly, the stereo, the sky box, dozens of CDs and videos. They did miss my daughter's jewellery, though. Apparently, the detective said that what they do is go in the bedroom and they draw the curtains and then they turn on the light and then they search the place. My daughter had her jewellery box on the window-sill and when they pulled the curtains, they obviously missed it. The insurance covered everything new for old and they were very good and asked how many CDs

I had and I could not remember so I plucked a figure out of the air. I said, with the box-sets, about one hundred and they paid up no questions asked. In a way, they did me a favour because all my gear needed upgrading and I couldn't afford it. I even got a new camera. The only provision they made was to improve the locks on the windows and if possible get a burglar alarm. A good friend of mine Rob just happened to be a fire alarm specialist and Doug was a burglar alarm specialist and his brother owned Sovereign Alarms. Between us we fitted a really nice alarm system.

I had many friends in the building trade and instead of just changing the locks, I decided to fit new windows. I hadn't fitted them before and it didn't look too difficult. I had seen them fitted before and I knew someone who made double glazing windows and with his help, we measured them and he delivered them. I forgot I had invited Rose over from Belgium. She was a bit down after Pauline's death and I thought a week with us might take her mind off it a little.

Saturday, I drove up to London to pick her up. I was up there and back by lunchtime. When we got back I had some of the scaffold built and she asked me what I was doing. I told her and thought that was that.

After a cup of tea and a natter, I said, "I just want to finish off the scaffold," and I went outside. I was struggling with a pole climbing up the outside and I got to the top and this voice called out and there she was, eighty-seven and passing a scaffold up to me.

On the Sunday, I had all the stuff in the front garden and so I decided I would fit them. They were two large bay windows finished by four o'clock.

I said to her, "I'll just tidy up," and then I heard a noise. I came out of the back garden and there she was pushing the scaffold from around the front and up the driveway. She really was an amazing woman.

That week, we showed her all around the sights and she loved it. Then I took her back to the station and I waved her off.

After we got back, I decided to finish the rest of the house. The little bedroom window at the front, the downstairs loo, and the shiplap on the front. I enjoyed doing something different and using the plastic and I decided to do the fascias, the soffits and replace the gutters and down pipes. After that, there was no painting, absolutely maintenance-free.

After that, the work came rushing in: next door wanted his windows done and his porch and his gutters and soffits, then two people over the road wanted theirs done. For a while, I got very busy.

As time went on I found it more difficult to work. My breathing was hard. The kids had all left home and Jackie and I were having problems keeping up the mortgage. We decided to downgrade, just along the road there was a flat for sale. It was ideal for what we wanted: two bedrooms, a large lounge and a new fitted kitchen. It was very light and airy with views over the downs and the airport and the other way over the sea. A nice balcony west-facing so you got the afternoon sun. It was on the second floor and we had no one above us and the neighbours were all very nice. We sold the house and bought the flat. Moving was not a problem, the hardest part was moving all my tools from one garage to another.

CHAPTER THIRTEEN

This day started like any other. I did a bit of work in the morning and in the afternoon I had an appointment up the Sussex County with the speech therapist who I knew very well. I had spent a few years learning to speak from my stomach. It works by swallowing air and bringing it back and using your throat to form words. I got quite proficient at this and people could understand me. I could even answer the phone. She put it to me that maybe I could speak better if I had a speaking valve fitted, a very small operation where they knock you out and then they put a hole in the back of your throat and insert a small plastic valve in the hole. It was about an inch and a half long. The only drawback was when it got blocked it had to be changed. This didn't bother me. I was used to putting all kinds of tubes down my throat, so I agreed.

My appointment came through very quick. And I went back to Sussex County. They said it would be a one day operation. We went up the theatre. They stuck a needle in my arm and the next thing I woke up in the ward. I saw the sign over my bed (Nil By Mouth). I was only allowed a sip of water now and again. They had these sticks with pink foam on the end like a large cotton bud and they would moisten your mouth with them.

That evening, I didn't get much sleep. The throat was coming to and was quite sore. The next morning, I sat there watching everyone eat their breakfasts. Later, the doctors came to do their morning rounds. They examined my throat and said everything was OK, and they went to the next bed, their entourage in tow.

They had just got to the other side of the ward when I felt really weird and giddy and I called the nurse and she came over and I told her how I felt. She said, "No wonder." My temperature had gone through the roof and my neck was swollen to three times its size. There was no way I was going home. They removed the valve, pumped me full of antibiotics and gradually I got better. They eventually let me home after two weeks. Apparently, I was allergic to the plastic that the valve was made of.

I was OK for a couple of years and then I started having a job to breathe. I went to the doctor's and he thought I had asthma and gave me reliever puffers. I took them for a couple of months but they did not help and so back up the Sussex County I went. I saw Mr Tranter again and he said he wanted me in again. They said they wanted to put a large camera down. They put me out and when I came too, they said my throat had closed and they could not get the camera down so he would have to operate. They would laser a piece off. This went very well and I was better in no time. What I didn't know was this was to happen at least twenty times over a period of two or three years. I actually made a point of going in every bed in Jowers Ward. I got to know everybody. All the nurses and volunteers and of course the patients, even the foreign cleaners.

One of the cleaners I had to report to the staff nurse. I was watching her and I could not believe what I saw: she was doing the floor and then she produced this filthy rag and started cleaning the bins. Nothing unusual there but then she went around with the same rag wiping people's water jugs. I never saw her on the ward again.

My mates still came up to see me and they would bring me up food (hospital food — yuck.) And they would tell me dirty jokes which all the nurses appreciated after I had cleaned them up a bit.

I must admit, I enjoyed hospital. I loved meeting new people. Some could be quite nasty and would have a go at the nurses at any opportunity. One in particular was having a go all day. In the end I had to go and sort him out. I explained they were not his slaves and there was more than him in the ward. I also explained they had brought him back from the dead twice. I told him to be nice to them or else they might have to do it a third time. After that, he was as good as gold. The nurses couldn't figure out why he was so nice; I never told them.

One evening I was lying there half asleep when there was this commotion and these two burly coppers brought in this fella in handcuffs. They stuck him in the bed next to me. I found out later he was on drugs. They handcuffed him to the bed and one copper sat with him all night; the following day, he was gone.

Many funny things happened. We had one fella who jogged and he would run through the ward and then go upstairs and you could hear him clunking across the ward upstairs. Well, he would do the circuit about about four times. They soon put a stop to that.

But I think the worst thing that happened was out on the balcony and this young doctor arrived and said he has to put a cannula in the back of my hand. It's a thick needle with a valve on it which they put different stuff in your blood stream through. Well, I swear he was only twelve years old. He tried to put this thing in my hand. After he had bent two needles, the visitor in the next bed said, "Give it here." He put it in straight away. (I later found out that this fella was a vet.) Anyway, I thanked him and the fella in the next bed and we ended up good mates. The doctor, however, I never saw again.

You had to go through Jowers Ward to get to Valance Ward and Valance was a surgical ward and had many very old patients and virtually every two weeks the nurses would pull all the curtains around our beds and you could hear this trolley come through the ward. One day, I had a peep through the curtains and I realised. They were taking out the ones that had popped their clogs. In the winter, this number would double.

Then came one of the hardest decisions I ever had to make. I was called up to the hospital one day and showed into this room. There were two doctors, a nurse and a speech therapist. They sat me down and then they brought me in a cup of tea. By this time, I was getting worried. Jackie was with me at the time and I could see she was getting worried. I thought the cancer had come back but thank god it hadn't. They explained they had lasered all they could. The options were to either leave it and after two years I would have to be permanently on oxygen or they could operate and do a laryngectomy. This of course meant they take away most of the back of my throat and disconnecting my nose and my mouth from my pipe that carries air to my lungs. This, in turn, meant a hole in my throat which I could breathe through.

It was quite an easy decision to make; I was not going to be strapped to an oxygen bottle for the rest of my life. I knew it was a big decision because they asked me on several occasions. This was probably one of the hardest things I had to decide on. The worst thing was no windsurfing, no water-skiing, no swimming and no showers because one spoonful of water in the hole in my throat and I'm a goner. I am even frightened to go out fishing in my mate's boat. Jackie and I had a couple of trips up to London and they took loads of X-rays and they gave me a date to go in. I was not looking forward to this as the Charing Cross hospital was quite a grotty place and I was concerned about Jackie travelling up there on her own because Charing Cross had quite a bad reputation for beggars, druggies and prostitutes especially around the station area.

I can't remember too much about my operation or the recovery. I do know when I came to I was in intensive care which was very frightening. I remember there were three beds and one other was occupied. There were banks of machines with lights and flashing screens. I also remember there was a nurse here full time monitoring and taking notes. Jackie was still there. Bless her. She had a worse job than me. I just laid there but she had to watch everything and she told me later there were times when she thought I would not make it. (Very hard for her.)

After a couple of weeks they moved me to a ward and after weeks later they let me go home. I know when we came home we were in a hospital car. I had a rubber tube up my nose which went to my stomach and when we got home we were greeted by the community nurse who explained how I had to plug a machine in for an hour and it would pump this foul-tasting liquid into my stomach. I had this contraption for a few months but I still managed to build a complete bedroom suite, cupboards, wardrobes and dressing table. It wasn't very easy dragging this machine about whilst drilling holes in the walls.

Eventually, this small hole in the back of my throat which was causing all of the trouble had healed up and I could drink without choking and I could eat normally. Also, this meant I could actually get out of the flat. The hole in my throat was about the size of a five-penny piece and my body treated it as an open wound. In time it would heal up. To prevent this, I learned to insert a pipe into it; this was bent at forty-five degrees and had two tags and a flange at one end to stop it going down your throat. The tags were attached to straps which did up behind your neck to stop you getting it caught up. The pipe was made of plastic but later I got a solid silver one. They didn't look very nice and so I wore a purpose-made bib and still do although I don't need the pipes any more. These pipes had to be taken out several times a day for cleaning. They would get blocked with phlegm. Now, I can cough it up in a tissue so it is no problem.

Sailing with Nick (K66).

I was registered as disabled but I still did little jobs for my friends and my kids. This operation had certainly slowed me down. I found it difficult doing the stairs to the flat.

I had to learn to speak again. This was so frustrating. We, as a group, often went to parties but no one could hear me. Even when we went for a meal someone would say something and I would have something to comment on but by the time I said it no one could so the moment had gone.

I would go over the beach and watch the lads windsurfing. This was great to watch but also on the other hand was heartbreaking and the thought that I could do this no more it actually made me cry. Windsurfing was a big part of my life. Even my clothes were surfing-inspired. I was very lucky. I managed to sell all of my gear to one person, a local builder. He was pleased and so was I but it was still painful loading my gear on the back of his van. It wasn't long after this kite surfing came out and the bottom fell out of second hand wind-surfing gear. You could not even give it away.

I still kept my hand in doing little jobs but I struggled to breathe and I was registered disabled. I still had trips up the hospital to see the speech therapist. The hole in my throat stopped trying to close and so I did away with the pipes. With just the bib I felt quite normal and the speech was getting better every day.

Then, one morning, I awoke and had this pain in my neck. I thought I had lain awkwardly. Anyway, this niggling pain would not go away. It slowly got worse. I went back to hospital a couple of times. They initially sent me to Southlands Hospital for physio. They were pushing and pulling and twisting my neck which made it hurt more. I tried heat pads and ice but nothing stopped it, not even the painkillers I was taking wholesale. One of my windsurfing mates recommended this chiropractor who had a place in Steyning. I made an appointment for the next day and Jackie and I went there.

She only had to feel my neck and said, "Brian you shouldn't be here, you should be in hospital. I will email them right away now."

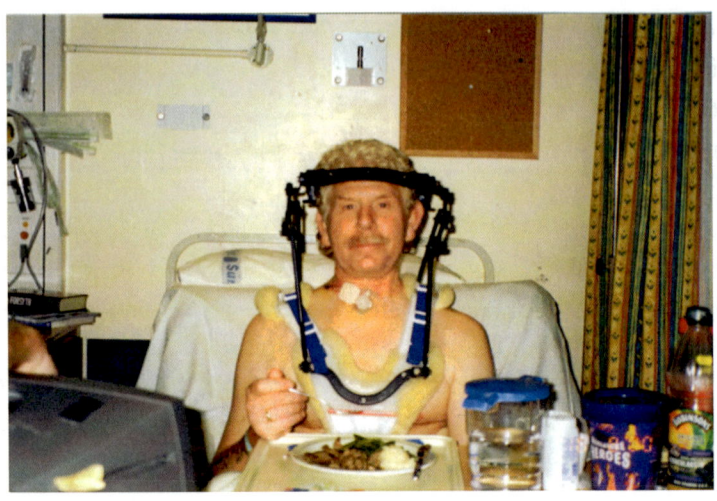

Because of my close involvement with the ENT in the Sussex County, I got a phone call when I got home and they wanted me in the next day. When I was upright, it was not too bad but if I tried to lie down the pain was so bad I could not hold back the tears. I had to sleep sitting up.

The following day, Mr Tranter and some other doctors had an examination of my neck and throat and then I went straight away in for a scan. They said they couldn't find anything but as a precaution they would fit a halo brace. For this, they had to put me out. We went up to the theatre and the next thing I woke up with this thing on my head. It was so heavy I had a job to move. I saw Jackie's face and so I made the effort and sat up. This thing sat on your shoulders. It had sheepskin padding on your shoulders and this big titanium cage which was bolted with five bolts to your skull. It stopped any movement in your neck. I had this thing on for a couple of weeks. Every two days they would come and tighten the bolts up. It was a strange feeling but it was not painful; they told me I would have to wear it for a couple of months. I would walk around the ward getting used to it. It was hard to get any clothes to fit around the frame. My mates who came to visit said if I still had it at Christmas they would decorate it, even with a set of fairy lights. The doctors said I would not be able to drive till it came off.

This particular day I had some visitors, Jackie as usual and Doug and Heather. Jackie had brought me a Cornish pasty and Heather had brought me some cakes. She worked in a cake shop. Jackie stayed on after Doug and Heather had gone home and I was sitting on the side of the bed just finishing a lump of homemade bread pudding.

I said to Jackie, "I need a wee."

I stood up and Jackie said she would come with me as you're a bit unsteady. I got halfway across the ward and my legs turned to jelly.

The ward sister was watching and said, "Don't muck about, Brian."

Well, I wasn't: my legs had gone and I collapsed to the floor. The nurses rushed over and got me back into bed. They called the doctors who did a few tests on me. They left and I sat on the bed chatting to Jackie. I didn't think it was a problem and Jackie went home. When I woke up in the morning, I could only move my head. The rest of my body was paralysed. I know I called the nurses over but after that things get a bit blurred.

Jackie was a rock; she was by my side all the time and she told me what had happened. I was transferred to Haywards Heath hospital; here my health seriously deteriorated. They operated on me immediately and they removed the halo on my head. Apparently, I had loads of visitors but I don't remember anyway. I remember Jackie but that was it. Keith, Allan and Chris all came up and left in tears; nobody thought I would get over this one. They pumped me full of morphine which in turn gave me the world's worst nightmares. I was frightened they would not know about the hole in my throat, the problem being I could not communicate and warn them about covering it up. One of the nurses did manage to shave off my moustache while I was asleep. I managed to get a deep vein thrombosis in both legs which swelled up like big balloons. They had to drain them and get rid of the deep vein thrombosis. They then told Jackie they would transfer me to Stoke Mandeville.

I was waiting for a bed for about a month, not that I remember much. I was still pretty much out of it. The day came and apparently they took me by ambulance and I have no recollection of the trip. The first thing I remember was coming to and realising I could not move from the neck down. I had pipes and tubes coming out of me everywhere. I could hear machines bleeping and buzzing. They had rigged up an angled mirror over my head so that people could see my face. I remember that three times a day they would stick a pipe down my throat and suck up all the fluid off my lungs: not very nice at all. Every few hours, they would call people from other wards into my room and they would very carefully turn me to prevent bed sores. And of course there were the injections; all the time injections.

The first time I saw Jackie I must have been really down because I told her to tell the doctors to turn everything off. I had had enough and wanted it all to end. I said this is not me lying here, fit and agile and good for a joke. I felt completely useless. We both cried. She explained to me I was being very selfish and I must confess when the kids came up it gave me a completely different outlook on life.

Jackie learned to lip-read very quickly. Although I could not move, I could feel certain things. I had terrible hypo sensitivity. The only way I could explain it, if anyone touched me even gently it felt like a million pins and needles or a high voltage electric shock. I still have it to this day but I manage it with drugs and willpower. Spasms were also very painful and uncontrollable. Something else I still have today.

After about two months of being in Stoke Mandeville I was still paralysed and Jackie came to visit and she said, "Do you mind if I don't come next week?"

I replied, "No I don't mind, why is that?"

She replied, "Alan, Doug and their wives want to take me to Spain for a week's break."

I smiled and said, "Of course I don't mind." (Under my breath I was saying, "Don't worry I will just lay here and die!" (Joke.)).

While I was in hospital in Brighton I met a fella who taught me to click with my mouth. I never realised how important this could be to me later in life. Because I was later lying there completely unable to move when the sister came into my room with a trainee nurse and told her to change the dressing on my throat. Well, off they went and a quarter of an hour later back came the nurse with a trolley and some bits and pieces on it. I watched her as she cut about three inches off this roll of plaster. She did not understand when I told her to stop so I started clicking. Thank god — just by luck the sister was passing and she yelled at the nurse who stopped. I hate to think what would have happened if she hadn't been passing.

Gradually, they started removing the pipes and tubes, until I just had two: one was a drain from the wound in my neck and the other was a catheter in my penis. I remember that this kept blocking and they decided to put it in my stomach; this is called a suprapubic catheter. This meant another small operation.

I was still being fed by this pipe up my nose but I had got used to this by now. Every week I would ask if I could have some real food and water, but the answer would always come back, 'not until the hole in the back of my throat had healed'. They would test this by giving me a drink of milk and watching if it leaked with an endoscope. This seemed to go on forever.

With the help of Dot, who was my physio, she was the top person of all the physios. I think she was the superintendent. Anyway, she got me moving my left arm one inch. It does not sound much but to me it was monumental. I felt if I could move that, I could move anything. Moving that inch enabled me to press a button which enabled me to call the nurse. The button was attached by velcro to my blanket. This, to me, was amazing. I vowed then to walk out of that place. Every day, the physios would come to the ward for an hour and manipulate my joints. The left hand side seemed to be easier than the right.

It wasn't until they sat me up and I looked in a mirror I could see even the right side of my face had dropped. I think this was more on my mind than the rest of my disabilities.

Time went very slowly but gradually I seemed to get a bit more mobile. I could, with my left arm, move it enough to scratch my head with one finger. One unpleasant memory I have was very early in the morning, about five, you would hear the rustle of a brown paper bag and you would lay there in anticipation: was it your turn or not? Then your curtains would part and your heart would drop to your boots. It was your turn. They would turn you on your side and with one rubber gloved finger would perform what they call 'manual evacuation'. Not very pleasant. I still cringe now when I hear the rustle of a brown paper bag.

Then one day, completely out of the blue, a doctor came around and said, "You can try a bit of dinner tonight." I was really looking forward to that. At five o'clock they came around and asked me what I wanted for dinner and I said, "Sausage, chips and beans."

When it came, it looked fantastic. I was sitting up and they put the tray on my lap. I asked for some tomato sauce. What a disappointment: I could only manage half a dozen mouthfuls. It tasted amazing but came up as quickly as it went down. It took quite a long time to get back to eating. As you progressed, you got to certain stages of repair and they would then move you to another ward. The strange part was the last ward you were in was closest to the front door.

Every couple of weeks, Karen would come visiting with Jackie and she was getting married very soon. She was quite upset because I could not give her away and I would miss the reception. They were going to hire a helicopter and fly to Stoke Mandeville. We have an airport at Shoreham. They even got the approval from Stoke Mandeville to use their heliport. But when it was worked out, it couldn't happen because the wedding was in the afternoon and it would have been too late because the helicopters at Shoreham will not fly when it's dark. Anyway, I got to see the photos the following week. She was disappointed, but that's life.

Showers in hospital were interesting. They would transfer you to a waterproof trolley that was painful with my hypersensitivity. They would cover you with a sheet and wheel you down to this big wet room. I would make sure my throat was covered and the nurses had great fun soaking me and each other.

Slowly, but surely, I began to move my right arm. I couldn't straighten it but I could move it. The fingers on my right hand wouldn't work. They said I might have to learn to write with my left hand. This was more difficult than I had anticipated.

By this time they said they would get me up. They turned up one morning with a hoist and a sling. At first, they were going to put me in a chair. They put the sling on me and then started to lift me. All I can say is the pain was excruciating. I had tears running down my face and I had to get them to stop. After that episode I had to have much more physio with Dot and next time they tried to lift me, the pain was just about bearable.

They put me in a chair. It felt so strange after being in bed for six months. I was also eating much better. I still had a drain in my neck and one morning they were taking me down to theatre to remove this and I blacked out. There was a big panic after that because they'd thought I had had a heart attack. It was something that had a special name which I can't remember. It put me on my back for another month with twenty-four hour nurse watch. But apparently it wasn't a heart attack.

Soon, I was back in my own ward and things progressed and before long, they had hoisted me into a wheelchair. This felt fantastic. I could use both hands and arms so I could propel myself around the ward, albeit very slowly. I had splints on both hands so it was a bit of a struggle. Also, my right arm would not straighten. They then decided to put it in plaster. It was very clever. Every week they would straighten it and stretch it then re-plaster it again and gradually it worked.

Meanwhile, they got me a powered wheelchair. I must have been the worst driver in the world, I crashed it in to everything. I was glad to get back in an ordinary wheelchair. I was still getting bed physio. But Dot came in one morning and said, "Come on, Brian, we are going down the gym today."

So they hoisted me into the chair and she had to push me because it was a fair distance away. When we went in, I could not believe my eyes. There were twenty-five people in there (all with different degrees of paralyses) and about fifteen physios, benches and specialised equipment all around. You did a lot of bench-work at first and then they got you standing.

They had a special machine for that, at first it was torture but gradually you could stand (strapped in) for quite a while and there were machines for strengthening your top half as well as your legs.

One day I was having a cup of tea and I happened to be watching CNN (an American news programme) when all of a sudden they switched to a picture of a plane crashing into a multi-storey block of offices. I thought I was watching a film they were going to ban or something; when I turned up the volume I realised what was happening. I called the nurses and before I knew it the whole ward was in there with me. The physios came up to see where I was and then got stuck like the rest of us; that's a day I'll never forget. Back in the gym the topic of everyone was nine eleven and in the restaurant in fact everywhere that was all people talked about.

After being in bed for many months, being hoisted into my wheelchair, they came into my room with this contraption; apparently it was a walking machine. You stood in it and held onto some handles. Well, I managed about ten steps and then collapsed into my wheelchair. Every day for that week I got better and better.

On the Sunday, Jackie, Keith and Sylvia turned up. I was in my wheelchair and I was about to go down to the kitchen to make some tea when Dot and the occupational therapist turned up. I asked what they were doing working on a Sunday, they replied "We have come in for a special reason" and with that they fetched in the walker. I got out of the wheelchair and started walking. It was the first time they had seen me walk. Jackie started crying, and then Sylvie, and that started Keith off! In the end, everyone shed some tears, even me. I did the length of the corridor and they were so pleased.

Back in the gym it seemed to go on forever, all the hard work paid off and gradually things got better. I started walking with a Zimmer frame; I could do a circuit of the gym. They told me we would be going out one day just to get used to all the outside noises and things after being in the hospital so long.

The day came and they said we would be going to Henley. It was a lovely day they pushed me in the wheelchair into the back of the purpose built van and off we went. It was so strange, thirty miles an hour felt like a hundred. We parked up in the town and went for a walk along the river bank. Everything looked so big, a Ready Mix lorry passed us and it seemed huge.

Lunchtime came and we went into this lovely old pub. We all had a slap up meal and I finished it off with a Scotch and coke. Dot was with us and an occupational therapist. I put my hand in my pocket and got out my wallet and they all said, "No! No! This is on Stoke Mandeville." I was amazed, it was a really nice day out. Sitting on the river bank eating an ice cream and chatting with two young ladies I was quite sad knowing we had to go back to the hospital. It wasn't too bad though because earlier I had asked about driving again and I had read about the modifications they could do for disabled drivers. They told me they had a date and it was in a week's time.

My left side was much stronger than my right and this showed up when we got there and they tested me. I remember they got me up very early that day, just tea and toast for breakfast and off we went. It seemed like miles away; eventually we arrived there and it was in a huge wood, there were proper roads and traffic lights. Anyway we went into this building and they did several tests and finally they said all I needed was a flip over throttle peddle. We then went around to the back of the building and they had all these adapted cars, some were amazing. They showed us a few that would suit my needs, with storage for my wheelchair. It was all very interesting. Finally he came over with a Ford Fiesta that had a left foot accelerator. It were an automatic so there was only two pedals.

He got out and said to me, "Get In." He then got in the passenger seat and said, "Take your feet off the peddles." I looked across and noticed it wasn't a dual control. He said to just drive like I would normally do.

I said, "What about the peddles?"

"Don't worry about that," he said and then he told me to start the car. He leaned with his walking stick and pressed the throttle and the brake. By the time we had done one circuit my nerves had calmed down, on the second circuit I had got used to it. We stopped and he said, "It's your turn with the left foot." I did a couple more circuits and it was no problem. He said there were no problems and I was OK to drive. I was really pleased, we filled in some forms and went to the front door. He shook my hand and I thanked him and then he said, "By the way, what's the registration of that car over there?"

I could hardly see the car. He then made me promise to get my eyes tested, they got in touch with DVLA and I finally got my driving licence back. This place where I took my test had miles of roads and apparently they rented it out to film companies and it had been used for quite a few James Bond films and quite a few war films, very interesting I thought.

We got back that evening just in time for dinner, which was appreciated and never touched the sides. I slept like a log that night, they even had a job to wake me next morning, it must have taken it out of me that day.

CHAPTER FOURTEEN

Routinely they would come round and test everybody for MRSA, there was a lot of press about it then. Anyway they came round one morning and said, "Brian, you have to go into an isolation room, which you are not allowed to leave, because you have MRSA." I had just started to go down to the gym at this time and so that had to stop. No one could come in the room without a mask and apron, everything from the room had to go into double red plastic bags; strangely enough this didn't apply to visitors. I had to have injections every day in my stomach, quite painful as I remember. My kids clubbed together and bought me a portable radio and CD player and I would play all my CDs all day. I think I may have said before but all the music piped all around the hospital were all those terrible pan pipes. The doctors when they came in would comment on the music, they said it was nice to hear after the constant pan pipes.

I was in this room for about a month, I think I was in there on my birthday because my son Paul brought me up a compilation CD he had put together. It was all records I liked and in between the tracks he had put a message from all of my mates and their wives. It was great and I still have it today.

The treatment for the MRSA seemed to go on forever but finally they came in and said I was clear and could go down the gym the next day. I thought, 'wonderful'. The following morning I got up, had a shower and breakfast and I was raring to go. I was first in the queue at the gym. I was strapped in the standing machine. I was only there twenty minutes when the ward sister appeared at the door. She pointed at me and I thought, 'What have I done wrong?'.

She came over and said, "Sorry, but you still have MRSA." My heart sank down to my boots. Back in the ward, I was not a happy bunny, I asked the sister what had happened and she said apparently although I was clear because I had stayed in my room I had caught it again, that meant another month in solitary.

Eventually I got clear and things went back to normal. They then decided to intensify my OT work, because of my hyposensitivity this was very painful. I had to plunge my hands into boxes of different things like dried peas, rice, small stones and sand; this was so painful it would make me cry. There was also things to improve your dexterity like nuts and bolts to assemble and things to thread. We also made special pushing gloves out of leather and of course they got me writing. My left hand side was not as bad as my right and so at first I tried to write with my left. I did manage it eventually. As my right hand improved I went over to using it, my right arm was fixed at forty degrees which made it very difficult to push my wheelchair and they decided they would strengthen it. They stretched it a little and then put it in plaster. With that on my arm it was impossible to push my chair and so they got me a motorised one. That was a bad mistake I think I crashed into everything and everyone possible, I was a liability. They would cut the plaster off every two weeks, bend my arm a little and re-plaster it again. This worked very well and now it is as straight as my left arm.

One time we had a sports day, it was held inside and outside. I wasn't strong enough to do much but I did win a medal for throwing the welly. It was amazing to see some of these disabled people go around the track on all of these specially converted cycles and wheelchairs. One I had never seen before was made for this fella, it was amazing. Somehow he had broken his back and the surgery meant he had to lay on his stomach. He had this trolley and it had wheelchair wheels on the front and casters on the back, so he could push the front wheels and really zip along. It was a really good fun day.

A really unfunny day happened shortly after that. They bought this treadmill, a very special one, it was about four feet off the ground. You had to go up a ramp to get on it and on the top was this gantry with a harness suspended from it. It would calculate your weight and lower you down with the right amount of pressure for your disability. It cost over a million pounds, so Mr Dickhead (me) volunteered to demonstrate it. When I went down to the gym there were doctors, nurses, men in white coats with clipboards and men in suits and ties. Up the ramp I went and I got out of my chair and they strapped me into the harness, so far so good. They pushed the button to raise me up, the harness tightened and then my bowels opened. I really wanted to die on the spot, even the press were there. They lowered me back in my chair and I made a hasty retreat, the most embarrassing thing in my life.

Jackie had been talking to a solicitor about compensation and they said I had a pretty good case. I believe our solicitor at the time was my ex's sister-in-law, who recommended a firm in Brighton who specialised in medical cases. As it happened they were really good as I will explain later. Meanwhile the physio and the OT carried on and the bowel training and getting used to having a catheter. This at first was inserted in my penis, this was very troublesome and kept blocking apart from being very painful. If not caught in time it can cause something to happen which can be fatal. This meant another operation and it was inserted in my stomach just below my naval, they called this a suprapubic catheter and I still have one today which has to be changed by the District Nurse every four weeks.

Gradually things got better, I got stronger, they put marks on the corridor floor and every day I would try to walk further and it was working. In the gym I was working harder and I got to know all of the other patients and staff. There were a couple of young lads who I would compete with, we were always trying to beat each other. They had walking frames but I had progressed to a pair of walking sticks and one day I was doing a couple of laps of the gym and I got to the part where they stored all the wheelchairs and one of the lads clipped the side of my walking stick and I went headlong into all the wheelchairs. There was a hell of a crash and the gym went silent. The physios came running over but would not let me move in case I had damaged my neck. When they got me up I had to have an x-ray and a visit to the consultant. Anyway everything was OK and I was told not to go so mad.

The next big problem were stairs; they knew I lived in a block of flats and would have to tackle two flights before they would let me go home. Before, when I was able, I could and would bound upstairs three steps at a time. Funnily the first time I tried I could only do three steps, it was so frightening and difficult, it was even worse coming down. I found it was easier using the handrail one side and my stick the other. Learning to do the stairs was probably the hardest thing I ever did in Stoke. The help and the encouragement you were given, still amazes me. Day after day I went on those stairs; I even had nightmares about them. Then one day however there we were at the top of the first flight. There was a chair on the landing and I sat down, when I looked around I was really frightened but they told me if I didn't go down I would have to do the next flight to get to the lift, so I gritted my teeth and came down. Over a period of time I could do two flights and walking with sticks became, not a doddle, but much easier.

The pain in my hands was getting more bearable; at one time I had two Chinese nurses looking after me. We had a lot of laughs and they wrote me two wonderful letters when they moved on. One of them made me a good luck macrame pendant which stills hangs in my porch at home. The other one was getting married in the hospital. I asked why at the hospital and she told me neither of them could ever go home again because although he was a doctor, he was Japanese and the two countries hated each other with a vengeance. Neither of their families would have anything to do with them. I remember when she moved on there were quite a few tears.

The dedication of these nurses was quite amazing, one of the nurses who looked after me, she was about twenty years old, had to do some really horrible jobs but she always had a smile on her face. I was chatting to her and she told me she had just passed her driving test and the next morning I happened to be in the car park when she pulled up in a new sports convertible Jaguar. Apparently her husband was a property developer, she was loaded and did not have to work at all. It's funny how some things stick in your mind. I had this staff nurse on the ward, he was a really nice guy and wasn't there for a month. I asked if he was on holiday and they said no, it was a very sad story. His son was seventeen and had been to a disco and was walking home and he got to a bridge when he was attacked by a gang of youths, who stole his phone but then they threw him off the bridge even though he could not swim. It took two weeks of searching to find his body. They caught the gang of yobs and they all got prison sentences. He came back to work but he was never the same.

Jimmy Saville, I met the main man many times and I never had a clue as to what was going on, in fact I was singing his praises for years, I know he raised forty million pounds for Stoke Mandeville but that all stands for nothing now. There were plaques and photos of him with Charles and Diana, the new Internet café was called 'Jimmy's', but I went up there the other week and there is not a trace of him anywhere.

CHAPTER FIFTEEN

On my sixtieth birthday I had a real treat. They knew I couldn't do the stairs to get up to my flat, so Jackie, Carol and Alan had arranged for me to go to their house and they had put a bed on the ground floor. I spent the weekend at their place. They had told all the friends and relations and they all popped in, it was a very good day. When I got back to the hospital they told me I would have to have an adjustable electric bed. Jackie made a few enquiries and ended up very worried again, they were over a thousand pounds and there was no way we had that much money kicking about. One of Jackie's mates was the wife of a windsurfing mate of mine. Well she knew a friend of a friend and her husband used the surf shop (Surfladle) on the beach and between them they raised enough money to buy two singles and two special mattresses. The shop ran a raffle and they got lots of donations, Teresa and Rick knew someone in the trade. I could not thank them enough, I really did want to go home.

I kept on working at doing those stairs it was hard work and eventually one day they said we could try my stairs at home. About a week later they wheeled me out to a car and

I transferred into the front seat. The driver was a male nurse and there was a physio and an occupational therapy nurse in the back. As we approached Shoreham they were amazed at how lovely it was with the river Adur and Lancing College and the houseboats on the river, all different colours, shapes and sizes and it felt so strange when we pulled up outside my flat. I had not seen it for eighteen months.

Jackie was there to meet us and said, "There is a nice cup of tea up there if you make it. I didn't have to be told twice, I attacked those stairs like they were the last eight feet of Everest.

With Danny outside the shop.

They were so pleased to see me do it and after about an hour's rest they checked out the rest of the flat. I had a raised chair in the lounge and a frame around the toilet, a special manger lifter in the bath which you inflated and it would lift you out of the bath. They said they could see no problem with me coming home. I was so pleased I decided to take them all out to lunch at what was once my local, providing I could get down the stairs incident free, no problem. We were soon at the Green Jacket and we had a drink and they said what was I eating and I said a rack of ribs and they all decided to have the same. The landlady didn't let me down and they all said they were the best they had ever had. We dropped Jackie off back home and headed back to Stoke Mandeville.

A week later they gave me a leaving date, it was in two weeks' time. Those two weeks were the longest of my life. Eventually the day arrived, it was a Saturday and Keith arrived with his wife Sylvia and Jackie. They came through to the ward and collected my bags and medication. There were a lot of goodbyes to make, a lot of tears and laughs, there was a big crowd to see me off. I picked up my sticks and walked through the ward and into the corridor and there was the entrance. Keith was there and took a few pictures and I walked to the car. I fulfilled my pledge to walk out of Stoke Mandeville, I was so elated I could not stop smiling all the way home. The journey seemed very quick and the stairs were no problem. Jackie, bless her, had arranged everything: the beds, the chair, the toilet, the whole lot; it was fantastic to be home. It was amazing to think that I was flat on my back, at death's door, paralysed from the neck down, yet here I was sitting in my lounge in my chair and drinking a cup of tea.

I still had a few problems but they were manageable. The first time Jackie tried to wash my hair we had quite a laugh, the bathroom in the flat was a bit small and when I pushed my chair in there, there was no room for Jackie and so we tried to lean me over the bath, which I managed, but Jackie still could not reach and in the end she took off her skirt and got in the bath, that was the only way we could do it.

I remember I had a nurse called Jenny, she was Scottish and into Formula One in a big way because of David Coultard. Anyway she was so loud, she had clompy shoes and when she came up the stairs of the flat you knew it was her coming and she spoke so loud that when I met my neighbours from downstairs they would say, "Hello Brian, I hear you've had your bowels open today." I had to go to Southlands, our local hospital, for check-ups and physio. My physio told me that my posture was very bad and that I walked with a hunch back and that she wanted me in to straighten my back, so back into hospital I went. I was told to forget all I had learnt and to start again. In the bed next to me was a feller, his name was Ron Hill, and we got on like a house on fire. He had suffered a stroke and was in there for physio. A few beds down there was Phil, he had a bad attitude problem and he would swear at the nurses because they would not take him out for a fag. In the ward opposite us was a right nutter, he was a gypsy or a traveller or something. He would brag about how he, with his catapult, stopped a gamekeeper from chasing him by putting a stone through his Land Rover door and smashing his windscreen. He kept his catapult with him and he would show it to us. Who in their right mind would take a catapult into hospital with them?

I also met Mary, Ron's wife, she was a case, always jolly and laughing, she knew everybody. Anyway, Ron and I were chatting and it turned out one of his close friends happened to be my ex-partner, Keith. He had never mentioned him, it was strange because I knew all of his friends and he knew all of mine. How our paths had never crossed I don't know. We became good friends and even holidayed together. Mary hit it off with Jackie and we had some times I will never forget.

The time in Southlands went very quick and I was soon home again walking upright I might say with my sticks. Home was very boring apart from the visits to the solicitors and the trips to the major hospitals for assessment; I even went to Bristol and Harley Street. I still had all the lads visiting me but it was difficult when they were still working.

One day I was visited by a social worker, a foreign lady, and she asked me if I would like to attend a day centre. I refused point blank, I did not want to go down there with all those sick people; little did I know. All my mates, Keith, Alan and Chris all said give it a try, you might even like it. Eventually I gave in and said I would try it. The day came and reluctantly with the social worker and Jackie we arrived at Glebelands Day Centre and we were greeted by a lady in her forties — blonde hair, good looking, nice figure and a lovely smile. She welcomed us, made me a cup of tea and I thought I can hear laughter and lots of people came up to me and introduced themselves. Some were severely disabled and I felt quite comfortable with it.

We were then shown around. The first stop was the Art room, that was the first time I met Peter Conly, a lovely man and very clever, a super artist. He showed me what people were doing. There were several painting and a group doing papermaché and another doing mosaic, everyone was talking and laughing. The next room they were doing soft craft. The ladies and men in there were making quilts, cushions, embroidery and loads of leather work like purses, handbags & belts. The next room was the wood work room. That was a hive of industry, they were sawing and banging it was great. They were making toys, bird boxes and tables, shelving and picture frames, even cutting glass. In there I met Lee, he was a nice feller and had a lot of knowledge. There was a hairdressers, a chiropodist and masseur, everything the clients needed. There was music and all the clients were so lovely, some had cerebral palsy, some had MS, some had had a stroke and were paralysed down one side and some were just old and went for the company. It was so enjoyable I could not wait for the following week to come.

Well it did and there I was sitting on the bottom step waiting for the bus to pick me up. Glebelands had three buses which would ferry people in. When we arrived we went in, chose what we wanted for lunch and paid for it, then you were at liberty to go to any group you fancied, they would always fit one more in.

Because I got on so well with Peter I went to the Art room and I started painting pictures, something I hadn't done since I was at school. I loved it. I got very interested in monochrome and in time I got to paint over thirty pictures which we framed and hung. They all sold with the money going to Glebelands. I developed a way of doing these pictures very cheap. I would use the reverse side of a square of hardboard which was nobbly and do the pictures with black and white emulsion. When finished they looked like they had been painted on canvas. The best one I did was one of my granddaughter which everyone wanted to buy but my son has it hanging in the girl's bedroom. I did do one on canvas of a Chinese girl's face and they sold that for fifty pounds.

I also loved working with Peter in the woodwork room, everyday it was a laugh a minute. We made a complete range of things from toys to bird tables, the toys we would paint in bright colours and then varnish them. We made dolls' houses, rocking horses, garages, games, almost anything they wanted. They paid for the materials and then they took them home; they were so pleased to have made something.

We had one feller, he had cerebral palsy as a child and was severely disabled. He could talk but was hard to understand and he was permanently in a wheelchair. He could only move his right arm and one finger and thumb. Well I was looking at a mitre saw. I took it to pieces and fixed it with two handles, one each end. He would grab one end with his finger and thumb and I would go around to the other side of the bench and I would grab the other end. I would push it back and forward and he would beam from ear to ear. He had no teeth and we would laugh like drains.

It was such a happy place, we had a lady in the soft craft room and she had had a stroke which had left her severely disabled. She had lots of problems talking — her name was Janice. She would make incredible soft toys and her forté was needlepoint, it was amazing the work she did.

There was another feller who was in a wheelchair and his name was John and like me he used to be a builder. He had never touched a sewing machine in his life before and he made a fantastic full size quilt. He used to say, "Not bad for a hairy arsed builder."

It was about this time I received an official looking letter from the NHS. I opened it and my jaw dropped, for what they had offered for my disability was seven thousand pounds. I rang my solicitor and she said she had also received the same letter.

I had never heard her swear before but she said, "They are having a f*****g laugh." She said to me this often happens, take no notice, ignore it. This made me feel much better.

It was also about this time they asked me at Glebelands if I wanted to be a volunteer as I was helping more people all the time. I agreed and have been one ever since (I do get a free lunch though). One young girl I used to help, her name was Kathy, had severe MS. She was a lovely girl but sadly a couple of years later I went to her funeral. I went to loads of funerals over the years, too many to remember.

I must put you right about Keith. There were two Keiths who were good friends, one I worked with, roof tiling and then we went through the fishing and water skiing days. We went back years, he was the one who brought Jackie up to Stoke Mandeville every other weekend. He even changed his car so that it was even easier for me to get in and out. The other Keith I had known ever since I was working with my father fifty-five years ago. We ended up as business partners and we still keep in touch.

Some of my artwork.

The staff at Glebelands told me that we had a new volunteer starting and he was going to teach in the woodwork room. I thought we are doing OK, why get someone new. When he arrived I showed him what we had in the woodwork room: the machines, the timber, the picture frames and the glass. Then we sat down and had a chat. First of all I found out he was a diabetic and had to inject three times a day and he asked me to keep my eye on him in case he forgot. He then told me his name was Jack Powell and he asked if I had heard of him. He was an antique restorer, a very wealthy man. He shipped containers full of antiques to the States and all over the world. He had shops all over the world, he even had a place in Jersey. The following day he brought in some photos of some of the stuff he had re-built and made, it was stunning. Some of the veneer inlays were brilliant, he had even done work in Buckingham Palace.

While we were talking I mentioned I had lived in Portslade. He said, "You should have heard of me, my factory was in Portslade down on the Seafront Road," and his name was on it in huge letters. He told me he had to sell up as he was not a well man but of course at home he got very bored and that's why he became a volunteer. Occasionally he would forget himself and think he was back in the factory but I soon put him straight; between us we turned out some beautiful stuff.

Jack and myself larking about at Glebelands.

When working in the Art room one day Fiona came in and said that she had entered us in a competition, between all the day centres in Sussex and it would be displayed at Worthing Museum. We did not have a clue as to what we were going to make. The instructor at the time was Mike, a lovely man who brought his dog to the centre and he was a brilliant artist. I found out later he was a local GP, anyway he was teaching us enamelling and said he would incorporate some in whatever we made. We were racking our brains as what to make. We had loads of bits and pieces left over from a project that we had dismantled, we had two circles of thick plywood and some eight foot lengths of copper pipe and some wire mesh and a roll of black material. What the hell could we make with that? Well we stood and looked for ages and it seemed so strange because it hit us both at the same time, a multi coloured cloak. We would make a frame out of the timber and pipes, cover it with the black material and the wire mesh and then we made over a hundred three inch copper squares which were then enamelled and then we drilled holes in the corners and riveted it to the wire mesh, it took ages to assemble. By the time it was half done it looked brilliant and it kept playing on my mind, what we could say it was for, a giant or something.

Then one evening I had this idea about a highwayman and I started to write a poem, something else I had never done before. It went like this:

DURRINGTON DAN

This is a tale of Durrington Dan
Worthing's most famous highwayman
Now Dan, he was a strapping fella
He was brave, he was not yeller
Big and strong, eight foot tall in his wellies
Some said it was the cakes but I think it was the jellies
One day when looking in the larder
He found no food, so he looked harder
Alas no food had he got
His wife and kids had scoffed the lot
So there and then he decided-off he went with his Cape and his mask
And I s'pose if they had been invented he'd probably have taken a flask
He set off to the old Sompting by-pass, where he demanded "Stand and deliver"
Where some smart alec shot him just missing his liver
While recovering at home later, he said with a smile and a joke
"I know what would have saved me, I'll make a METAL CLOAK"
So he set to work weaving, using steel, brass and copper
He knew to keep the bullets out it would have to be made proper
When finished it looked the business, it gleamed and brightly shone
Mind you, it was pretty heavy when he finally got it on

When he went out in the dark nights robbing the wealthy gentry
He came back with loads of loot, gold and jewels aplenty
Bullets were flying everywhere and never got him ever
He got quite big headed, thinking he was so clever
Thinking he would expand his business, he trundled down to Goring
He found there were no rich men there, in fact it was flipping boring
He ended up a wealthy man with loads of jewels and cash
He'd sew some onto his metal cloak, well he'd give it a bash
He went down to Lancing, lots of rich people there
When they saw his amazing cloak, they couldn't help but stare
One day while counting his money, he found it really a bore
He had an idea (not one of his best) I'll give some of it to the poor
Then someone told him about the hard up, who lived on Shoreham beach
They had rags on their backs, no shoes on their feet, money to them was out of reach
So he filled up a bag with some money and staggered down to the boat
He started to cross the river, the flipping thing would only just float
By the time he got to the middle, the boat was leaking (no joke)
It wasn't the gold in his bags, it was the weight of his cloak
He sank to the bottom (bless him) he was really quite a nice bloke

When he drowned it wasn't the gold in his pockets, it was his life saving cloak
They dragged the river up and down, but alas to their dismay
The metal cloak was all they found, poor Dan had washed away
The Moral of this story is…
When in a boat don't rock it. Give your spare cash to charity.
Don't keep it in your pocket

This was done with one finger on my computer, I amazed myself. When I went back to Glebelands they thought it was great and so we framed it and it stood alongside the cloak when we exhibited at Worthing. We also had some breeze blocks which I carved to resemble a tombstone, which was placed inside the half open cloak. Even though I say it myself it was fantastic. I even had people asking me if Durrington Dan was a real person, even the Mayor of Worthing asked if he was a real person.

At Worthing Town Hall with cloak and poem.

The cloak.

CHAPTER SIXTEEN

As I mentioned before we had lots of trips to London for assessments and one day my solicitor said we have a meeting at their place in Brighton. When we went, in there were all these people sat around this large table and in the middle was an open phone. They were all discussing me: there was also a specialist on the phone. After half an hour it stopped and went very quiet and someone from the NHS said we will make an offer of nine hundred and fifty thousand pounds. It did not sink in at first, I looked at my solicitor and she looked at me and nodded and so we agreed.

On the way home Jackie still could not grasp what had just happened, I explained to her that with the flat we were millionaires. I felt quite light headed. When we got home we sat down and talked about it, it still felt very unreal. Later in the day my Brighton solicitor rang and said I must find a solicitor. I told them I already had one in Worthing. We rang them and made an appointment to see them the next day. I explained to Jackie she could have virtually anything.

The next day we went down to see them, we went in and took a seat. We explained to the girls behind the desk that we had an appointment and sat there waiting and waiting.

This girl came out with two cups of tea, I thought great but she gave them to the girls behind the desk. Eventually this fella came out and took us into this box room. We explained we wanted to make a will and he then asked us about our finances. He could see I was disabled and I told him I just had my disability money and Jackie said she was a hairdresser and didn't get a lot, and then he asked about pensions. I said I hadn't any, I said I was still paying the mortgage on the flat and he looked really disinterested. He then asked if I had any savings. I said none. He then started writing, after ten minutes he looked up at me and I said I have just had some compensation. He asked how much and when I told him his face lit up and he said sorry and showed us into another much bigger room. The next thing, the same young girl came in and asked us if we wanted tea or coffee. Out it came in bone china cups, I could not believe the different attitude money made.

We were there a couple of hours. We sorted out the wills and then we went home. We sat down and realised just what we had. I was still at Glebelands and so I spoke to Jack and he recommended his financial adviser. We gave him a ring and he agreed to come and see us, his name was Tony and he was very good. This was a completely new world and something I didn't understand. Portfolios and pieces of cheese and investments left me cold and went straight over my head. We explained we would like to give the kids some money, and to buy a bungalow and he said that was no problem, go out and spend. He said what we had invested made enough to live on. That was then, a bit different now.

I was still a service user at Glebelands and really enjoying it, when one day who should turn up but Ron who I had met at Southlands. There was Peter, Jack, Ron and myself, honest to God I have never laughed so much in my life. There were dirty jokes and wind ups galore. One in particular I remember was, we had a lady volunteer who came in and did the teas and things. Pam was her name and one day she came in the woodwork room and she remarked on the fact that she had to go to the hospital about her eye. Jack said there was no need to worry as he had a glass eye and it did not bother him. He asked her to take a closer look and see if she could tell which one it was. She had a long look and then she said, "Oh! Yes, it's your left one."

There was nothing wrong with his eyes he had perfect sight but we kept this going for months. The other thing we kept going for ages was the fact that we were gay and we were going to get rid of our wives and get married; this went right around the centre.

Another strange thing that happened was, we had this girl started as a volunteer (Jo), she would do the teas and generally help around the centre. About this time I was doing my paintings and she bought about three of them. She told me her son was a vet out in Australia and that he worked with Steve Irwin and the crocodiles. She told me she had the first edition of Lord of the Rings and I believed it all. It sounded quite plausible until I saw the Antiques Roadshow and one on there sold for three hundred thousand pounds. It was all lies, I think she believed them herself. Jackie at that time worked in Lancing and because we only had one car I would take her to work before going to Glebelands. I would then pick her up and bring her home in the afternoon. Well I passed Jo's house and so I would give her a lift in and home. This went on for a couple of months and then she started telling people she was getting married and her husband to be had bought a thatched cottage in Steyning.

One week I was on holiday and she would come on one of our buses and when I got back Roy the driver took me to one side and said, "You crafty old bugger."

I said, "What do you mean?"

He said, "You and Jo."

I said, "I don't understand." He said one morning she was late and he went in her place and was surprised to see photos of me all over the place and she was telling people that I was marrying her. She had even been accepting wedding presents off some of our service users. When I finally saw her I asked her what the game was. She went bright red and left the room, got her coat and that was the last I saw of her, thank god.

Now let me tell you about Ron, he was a lovely, lovely man. He had suffered a stroke which had left him severely disabled; his left arm was paralysed and his left leg did not work properly so he walked with a limp. He had a brilliant mind and he laughed like a drain. He was married to Mary and had a couple of grown up boys. Over the years we got very friendly and we would go on holiday twice a year to Tenerife. He knew it very well because at one time he had an apartment there. We had so many laughs.

While at Glebelands he wrote his life story, I remember him sitting in the computer room writing it with one finger. When he finished it he actually got it published (it was called Cheating the Grim Reaper). Sadly he was diagnosed with cancer and after a few months he died. Meanwhile we had so much fun going on holiday to Tenerife, he had a timeshare there once and so he knew the place very well. We would hire two electric buggies and race everywhere. The locals would say "Here comes Schumaker and Button." Los Americas was so wheelchair friendly with drop curbs and tiled promenades. We would stop off at a bar and have a beer or sangria, or a Shangrila, as Jackie would say. We would do a lot of people watching. One day we were sitting in a bar and two young local lads came along, they were carrying a large boat's fender it was fluorescent pink and a blow up type made of hard rubber. The next thing they did was to dig a hole in the sand, they buried half of it and left half exposed, it was intriguing, we sat and watched as did everyone else. When they finished they took a run up and used this thing as a spring board and did these amazing double summersaults and swallow dives into a forward roll. When they finished people were giving them money, I think they did quite well, very entrepreneurial.

Jackie and Mary would do the shops and we all had quite a time. I still miss him greatly. This affected me quite a bit and something from forty years ago when I first got cancer kept ringing in my ears, it was Mr. Tranter saying, "If there is anything you want to do, then do it." I had always wanted to see America and so we talked to Jackie's brother and decided to go. We had been on holiday with him and his partner, Carol, before. We went to Rhodes and had a cracking good time, and so we went to New York and then on to Las Vegas, and what a holiday that was. New York was an experience, we did the normal things like the Empire State Building and Central Park in an open top horse drawn carriage and we also went in the Hard Rock Café, they have famous guitars hanging on the walls and a couple Grayham (Jackie's brother) had worked on. We went to Time Square and went in Toys R Us and it was quite incredible to see a full size ferris wheel inside the store and it was working.

New York was very impressive but three days was not enough time to see it all. Being in a wheelchair, the hustle and bustle was quite uncomfortable, like London, everybody in such a rush. We did get to visit the Nine Eleven site but that's what it was a huge building site. Three days just flew by and before we knew it we were on the plane to Vegas. Even though it was an internal flight the customs were so thorough, everyone had gone and were waiting for me. I thought they were going to take my wheelchair apart. Finally they let us in, it was a limo to the hotel. When we arrived the hotel was shaped like a pyramid; it was strange to see the lifts going up sideways, mind you everything was strange, incredible, something I will never forget.

We managed to see a show (Lion King) not my cup of tea. I would have rather seen Celine Dion but she finished the week before we arrived, just my luck. The casinos were amazing, much too much to describe, they say it's like Disneyland for grown ups and it is definitely true —

everything is OTT. Like we went to one casino and could not understand what was happening at the back of this place, so we went over to have a look. They had constructed a sunny beach with sand parks, trees and sun beds, even brollies and little waves breaking on the beach. Very good you might say but the water went up to a glass wall which was in fact a huge aquarium and in there were many sharks. In the tank was a large clear perspex tube, I wondered what it was for. I soon found out, someone came sliding through, it was part of a water slide. And of course we had to do the Grand Canyon, for me it was the icing on the cake. Jackie was not too pleased when she found out we were going on a helicopter, she was not keen on aeroplanes. Grayham and Carrol kept telling her it was OK, she was really frightened. Anyway we got her in the helicopter and I could see she was not a happy bunny but the minute we lifted off she completely changed, she absolutely loved it. We went down to the bottom and refuelled and were able to get out and have a look around it was amazing, I think the expression is mind blowing.

We did meet up with a couple of friends of ours, Andy and Sylvia who lived there. They showed us around lots of places we would never have found, Old Vegas was truly something special, on the hour every hour they had a laser light show on the ceiling, hundreds of yards long, it was all split up into bays and each one had something different going on. Some had bands, some had solo singers and some had artists doing portraits, it was just a magical experience.

Before I bore the pants off you I must tell you about the last one I had, we went to Minorca, a lovely hotel with the obligatory pool. Just minutes away was a lovely bay, sandy beach with sunbeds, they had a wooden path down to the water's edge which was ideal for me in my scooter I had hired. We got some sunbeds, I was amazed at how blue the sea was and how shallow it was, and bearing in mind I had not been in the sea for twelve years, I decided I would go for a paddle if I could. With Grayham and Carrol's help I walked a few feet down the sand and went for my paddle, it was great I was so chuffed. Anyway the following day Jackie and me went down to the bay and decided to have a drink at the bar. Well we got talking to this fella and his wife and in the conversation I mentioned that I was so pleased I had been for a paddle and how much I would have loved to actually get in the sea and he said I could, I said I couldn't because I had a hole in my throat which went to my lungs, just a small drop of water in there could kill me. He insisted I still could. He said at the Red Cross place back down the beach they had a contraption that would get me in the water; we thanked them.

On the way home we were both bemused and so we popped in the Red Cross and they showed us this wheelchair that went in the sea. It had floats built in and had fat tyres to go over the sand, they said to come in tomorrow and we agreed. Next day, unfortunately our last day, we all went to the beach and we went into the Red Cross and they would be along shortly. They turned up about half an hour later with this contraption. They helped me into it there were no straps or a belt even, I just had to hang on to two handles. They slowly pushed me in the sea, I must admit I was terrified I was holding on like grim death, this was a real white knuckle ride, the further in we went the higher the water got. Well it got to my chest and we suddenly started floating. They transferred the handles to Grayham and I began to like it, I relaxed and began enjoying it. I must say the whole experience did not seem real, it was me in the sea after all those years. I enjoyed it so much when we got back we rebooked the holiday.

I did have some fantastic birthday treats, organised by Jackie, Karen and the boys. I did a helicopter trip in a tiny two seater, that was quite an experience. We got back a bit early and he was told to waste ten minutes so he took me over my flat and then he followed the river down to the lock gates and then the power station. He then laid it on its side and I could see down inside the chimney. As it was the cockpit of these machines is so small one shoulder is touching the pilot and the other shoulder is hard against the window and it swings about under the blades, quite exciting.

Then I did the racing car experience, we went to Thruckston race track, which just happens to be the fastest track in the country. When we arrived I had to get into a racing suit including a crash helmet. The first one was quite breathtaking. It was a Mazda saloon and I kept thinking, he is not going to make this bend. I did three circuits and then we came back in the pits and we then went out in a Porsche and we passed the Mazdas like they were standing still.

About half an hour later they came over and asked me if I was sure I wanted to do the true racing car, I of course said, "Too true I do." The fellas there were so helpful. Anyway one of them helped me into this motor and you had to buckle into a full racing safety harness, when he pressed the button this machine burst into life. Seriously this thing rattled like a bag of nails and it shook violently. He let out the clutch and we took off burning rubber for fifty yards, it had a digital speedo but you were shaking so much it was difficult to read. We passed Porches one after another, man that thing was fast down the straight we were doing one hundred and sixty miles per hour. All the time he was casually talking to me about how he loved summer and the girls in their short skirts. Anyway we got held up on one lap and so he took me on an extra lap. When we came to a halt the fella who helped me get in came over to help me get out. He asked the driver how I did and he replied, "He is one cool dude." That made my day.

My most recent trip was a flight in a Tiger Moth but I was a little disappointed because apparently they said I would not be able to get in it. I went up in a Piper, a small four seater. On the way down to Chichester he told me what to do and he let me take over the controls, really exciting. I'm still here and so you can see I didn't crash it. My walking is still limited to forty yards.

CHAPTER SEVENTEEN

I feel so privileged to be able to do these things, when I think back to how I was.

I remember coming back home from holiday to Gatwick one time and the flight had been delayed. Ron and I were both in wheelchairs and the pilot had radioed through for assistance; disabled people always get off the plane last anyway. Well they had all gone and we were sitting there with the crew waiting and waiting, they were not too happy because they wanted to go home and of course they couldn't till we went. After about three quarters of an hour the assistance truck turned up. We got on it, it lowered us down and off we went. We got to the terminal and they rushed us through. We were in the lounge when this official looking fella came over to us and explained we were at the wrong terminal. We were bundled back through customs, up and down in lifts, down long corridors, back to the bus which took us to terminal two, back through customs, more lifts, more corridors and we arrived at the carousel and of course, no cases. Eventually we found them; they had been taken off and stashed in a corner. Meanwhile our driver had been waiting for us and had been around the airport half a dozen times, I think in the end we were two hours late and well pissed off.

Ron's one fault was he had an anger management problem. He was OK most of the time but occasionally he would kick off. I was really proud of myself because I taught him to count to ten first and it seemed to work. I must admit I really miss old Ron, we still keep in touch with Mary though.

A couple of years back Glebelands went over to Mental Health and now we deal with customers with alzheimers and dementia. It can be very hard work and sometimes we have a laugh but it is so rewarding and I love it.

My book is coming to a close now but I would like to thank my closest friends, Keith Lambert, Alan Smith, Chris Bunby, Keith Addison and their wives, for all their support over the years. And of course the family — Colin, my brother, the children Paul, Karen, Graham and Emma and the grandchildren, for the fun they have given me. And last but not least my darling wife Jackie. She has been a brick, it must have been harder for her than it was for me and I suppose still is. Without her I don't think I could have made it. She does my medication, my dressings, my baths and runs the house and we still laugh together. She has sorted all my appointments at the hospitals, she waits on me hand and foot. If anyone deserves a medal, it's her. In my eyes she is a saint and I love her to bits.

Well that's it — the real life of Brian at seventy three. I wouldn't have changed a thing.